What They're Saying about "They Say / I Say"

"This book demystifies rhetorical moves, tricks of the trade that many students are unsure about. It's reasonable, helpful, nicely written . . . and hey, it's true. I would have found it immensely helpful myself in high school and college."
—**Mike Rose**, *University of California, Los Angeles*

"Brilliantly simple . . . adds to the argumentative strategies students already possess . . . distills the essence of academic discourse in a way that students can understand and employ in their own writing."—**Russel Durst**, *University of Cincinnati*

"I absolutely love the governing idea of this book. As a teacher and WPA, I'm constantly thinking about how I can teach my students—and how I can help instructors teach their students—to make specific rhetorical moves on the page. This book offers a powerful way of teaching students to do just that."
—**Joseph Bizup**, *Columbia University*

"The ability to engage with the thoughts of others is one of the most important skills taught in any college-level writing course, and this book does as good a job teaching that skill as any text I have ever encountered."
—**William Smith**, *Weatherford College*

"I like the way Graff and Birkenstein pick apart what's really happening in an argument. Many students get to college not knowing how to make the moves necessary to put forth an argument, and this book helps them work through that process."—**Christine Cozzens**, *Agnes Scott College*

"The argument of this book is important—that there are 'moves' to academic writing . . . and that knowledge of them can be generative. The template format is a good way to teach and demystify the moves that matter. I like this book a lot."—**David Bartholomae**, *University of Pittsburgh*

"A joy to read . . . like having a private tutorial with gifted teachers."
—**Sarah Duerden**, *Arizona State University*

"Especially for beginning writers, 'They Say / I Say' offers an excellent roadmap to the new world of academic discourse."
—**Daniel Zimmerman**, *Middlesex County College*

"Graff and Birkenstein's basic argument is both persuasive and congruent with my own experience: these are the moves I needed to learn as a student. A very, very smart book."—**Lisa Ede**, *Oregon State University*

CONTENTS

—◻—

INTRODUCTION

"THEY SAY / I SAY"

The Moves That Matter

in Persuasive Writing

"THEY SAY / I SAY"

The Moves That Matter

in Persuasive Writing

—▭—

GERALD GRAFF

CATHY BIRKENSTEIN

both of the University of Illinois at Chicago

W · W · NORTON & COMPANY

NEW YORK   LONDON

For
Aaron David

Copyright © 2007 by W. W. Norton & Company, Inc.

All rights reserved
Printed in the United States of America

The Library of Congress has cataloged another edition as follows:
Graff, Gerald
    "They say/I say": the moves that matter in academic writing / Gerald
    Graff, Cathy Birkenstein.
    p. cm.
    Includes bibliographical references and index.
    ISBN-13: 978-0-393-92409-1 (pbk.)
    ISBN-10: 0-393-92409-2 (pbk.)
    1. English language—Rhetoric—Handbooks, manuals, etc. 2. Persuasion
    (Rhetoric)—Handbooks, manuals, etc. 3. Report writing—Handbooks,
    manuals, etc. I. Birkenstein, Cathy, II. Title.

PE1431.G73 2006
808'.042—dc22

                                                              2006040818

ISBN-13: 978-0-393-06545-9 (cloth)

W. W. Norton & Company, Inc., 500 Fifth Avenue, New York, N.Y. 10110
                        www.wwnorton.com

W. W. Norton & Company Ltd., Castle House, 75/76 Wells Street,
London W1T 3QT

        5 6 7 8 9 0

PREFACE

Demystifying Academic Conversation

—⌑—

EXPERIENCED WRITING INSTRUCTORS have long recognized that writing well means entering into conversation with others. Academic writing in particular calls upon writers not simply to express their own ideas, but to do so as a response to what others have said. The mission statement for the first-year writing program at our own university, for example, describes its goal as helping students "enter a conversation about ideas." A similar statement by another program holds that "intellectual writing is almost always composed in response to others' texts." These statements echo the ideas of rhetorical theorists like Kenneth Burke, Mikhail Bakhtin, and Wayne Booth as well as recent composition scholars like David Bartholomae, Patricia Bizzell, Peter Elbow, Joseph Harris, Andrea Lunsford, Elaine Maimon, Gary Olson, Tilly Warnock, Mike Rose, and others who argue that writing well means engaging the voices of others and letting them in turn engage us.

Yet despite this growing consensus that writing is a social, conversational act, helping student writers actually "enter a conversation about ideas" remains a formidable challenge. This book aims to meet that challenge. Its goal is to demystify academic writing by isolating its basic moves, explaining them clearly, and representing them in the form of templates. In this way, we hope to help students become active participants in the important conversations of the academic world and the wider public sphere.

HIGHLIGHTS

- *Shows that writing well means entering a conversation*, summarizing others ("they say") to set up one's own argument ("I say").
- *Demystifies academic writing*, showing students "the moves that matter" in language they can readily apply.
- *Provides user-friendly templates* to help writers make those moves in their own writing.

HOW THIS BOOK CAME TO BE

The original idea for this book grew out of our shared interest in democratizing academic culture. First, it grew out of arguments that Gerald Graff has been making throughout his career that schools and colleges need to invite students into the conversations and debates that surround them. More specifically, it is a practical, hands-on companion to his recent book, *Clueless in Academe: How Schooling Obscures the Life of the Mind*, in which he looks at such conversations from the perspective of those who find them mysterious and proposes ways in which such mystification can be overcome. Second, this book grew out of writing templates that Cathy Birkenstein developed in the 1990s, for use in writing and literature courses she was teaching. Many students, she found, could readily grasp what it meant to summarize an author, to support a thesis with evidence, to entertain a counterargument, or to identify a textual contradiction, but they often had trouble putting these concepts into practice in their own writing. When Cathy sketched out templates on the board, however, giving her students some of the language and patterns that these sophisticated moves require, their writing—and even their quality of thought—significantly improved.

This book began, then, when we put our ideas together and realized that these templates might have the potential to open up and clarify academic conversation. We proceeded from the premise that all writers rely on certain stock formulas that they themselves didn't invent—and that many of these formulas are so commonly used that they can be represented in model templates that students can use to structure and even generate what they want to say.

As we developed a working draft of this book, we began using it in first-year writing courses that we teach at UIC. In classroom exercises and writing assignments, we found that students who otherwise struggled to organize their thoughts, or even to think of something to say, did much better when we provided them with templates like the following.

▶ In discussions of _____, a controversial issue is whether _____. While some argue that _____, others contend that _____.

▶ This is not to say that _____.

One virtue of such templates, we found, is that they focus writers' attention not just on what is being said, but on the *forms* that structure what is being said. In other words, they help students focus on the rhetorical patterns that are key to academic success but often pass under the classroom radar.

THE CENTRALITY OF "THEY SAY / I SAY"

The central rhetorical move that we focus on in this book is the "they say / I say" template that gives our book its title. In our view, this template represents the deep, underlying structure, the internal DNA as it were, of all effective argument. Effective persuasive writers do more than make well-supported claims ("I say"); they also map those claims relative to the claims of others ("they say").

Here, for example, the "they say / I say" pattern structures a passage from a recent essay by the media and technology critic Steven Johnson.

> For decades, we've worked under the assumption that mass culture follows a path declining steadily toward lowest-common-denominator standards, presumably because the "masses" want dumb, simple pleasures and big media companies try to give the masses what they want. But . . . the exact opposite is happening: the culture is getting more cognitively demanding, not less.
>
> STEVEN JOHNSON, "Watching TV Makes You Smarter"

In generating his own argument from something "they say," Johnson suggests *why* he needs to say what he is saying: to correct a popular misconception.

Even when writers do not explicitly identify the views they are responding to, as Johnson does, an implicit "they say" can often be discerned, as in the following passage by Zora Neale Hurston.

> I remember the day I became colored.
>
> ZORA NEALE HURSTON, "How It Feels to Be Colored Me"

In order to grasp Hurston's point here, we need to be able to reconstruct the implicit view she is responding to: that racial identity is an innate quality we are simply born with. On the contrary, Hurston suggests, our race is imposed on us by society—something we "become" by virtue of how we are treated.

As these examples suggest, the "they say / I say" model can improve not just student writing, but student reading comprehension as well. Since reading and writing are deeply reciprocal activities, students who learn to make the rhetorical moves represented by the templates in this book figure to become more adept at identifying these same moves in the texts they read. And if we are right that effective arguments are always in dialogue with other arguments, then it follows that in order to understand the types of challenging texts assigned in college, students need to identify the views to which those texts are responding.

Working with the "they say / I say" model can also help with invention, finding something to say. In our experience, students best discover what they want to say not by thinking about a subject in an isolation booth, but by reading texts, listening closely to what other writers say, and looking for an opening in which they can enter the conversation. In other words, listening closely to others and summarizing what they have to say can help writers generate their own ideas.

THE USEFULNESS OF TEMPLATES

Our templates themselves have a generative quality, prompting students to make moves in their writing that they might not otherwise make or even know they should make. The templates in this book can be particularly helpful for students who are unsure about what to say, or who have trouble finding enough to say, often because they see their own beliefs as so self-evident that they need not be argued for. Students like this are often helped, we've found, when we give them a simple template like the following one for entertaining a counterargument (or planting a naysayer, as we call it in Chapter 6).

▶ Of course some object that _____. Although I concede that _____, I still maintain that _____.

What this particular template helps students do is make the seemingly counterintuitive move of questioning their own beliefs, of looking at them from the perspective of those who disagree. In so doing, templates can bring out aspects of students' thoughts that, as they themselves sometimes remark, they didn't even realize were there.

Other templates in this book will help writers make a whole host of sophisticated moves that they might not otherwise make: summarizing what someone else says, framing a quotation in their own words, indicating the view that the writer is responding to, marking the shift from a source's view to the writer's own view, offering evidence for that view, entertaining and answering counterarguments and explaining what is at stake in the first place. In showing students how to make such moves, templates do more than organize students' ideas; they help bring those ideas into existence.

OKAY, BUT *TEMPLATES*?

We are aware, of course, that some instructors may have reservations about templates. Some, for instance, may object that such formulaic devices represent a return to prescriptive forms of instruction that encourage passive learning or lead students to put their writing on automatic pilot.

This is an understandable reaction, we think, to kinds of rote instruction that have indeed encouraged passivity and drained writing of its creativity and dynamic relation to the social world. The trouble is that many students will never learn on their own to make the key intellectual moves that our templates represent. While seasoned writers pick up these moves unconsciously through their reading, many students do not. Consequently, we believe, students need to see these moves represented in the explicit ways that templates provide.

The aim of the templates, then, is not to stifle critical thinking but to be direct with students about the key rhetorical moves that comprise it. Admittedly, no teaching tool can guarantee that students will engage in hard, rigorous thought. Our templates do, however, provide concrete prompts that can stimulate and shape such thought: What do "they say" about my topic? What would a naysayer say about my argument? What is my evidence? Do I need to qualify my point? Who cares?

In fact, templates have a long and rich history. Public orators from ancient Greece and Rome through the European Renaissance studied rhetorical *topoi* or "commonplaces," model passages and formulas that represented the different strategies available to public speakers. In many respects, our templates echo this classical rhetorical tradition of imitating established models.

In our own day, the journal *Nature* offers aspiring contributors a templatelike guideline for the opening page of their manuscripts: "Two or three sentences explaining what the main result [of their study] reveals in direct comparison with what was thought to be the case previously, or how the main result adds to previous knowledge."

In the field of education, a form designed by the education

theorist Howard Gardner asks postdoctoral fellowship applicants to complete the following template: "Most scholars in the field believe _____ . As a result of my study, _____ ." That these two examples are geared toward postdoctoral fellows and advanced researchers shows that it is not only struggling undergraduates who can use help making these key rhetorical moves, but experienced academics as well.

Templates have even been used in the teaching of personal narrative. The literary scholar Jane Tompkins devised the following template to help student writers make the often difficult move from telling a story to explaining what it means: "X tells a story about _____ to make the point that _____ . My own experience with _____ yields a point that is similar/different/both similar and different. What I take away from my own experience with _____ is _____ . As a result, I conclude _____ ." We especially like this template because it suggests that "they say / I say" argument need not be mechanical, impersonal, or dry, and that telling a story and making an argument are more compatible activities than many think.

WHY THE "I" TABOO IS MISTAKEN

But wait—"as a result, *I* conclude"? "They say/*I* say"? How can we so flagrantly encourage the use of the first-person pronoun? Aren't we aware that many English teachers prohibit their students from using "I" or "we," on the grounds that these pronouns encourage ill-considered, subjective opinions rather than objective and reasoned arguments? Yes, we are aware of this line of reasoning, but we think it has serious flaws. First, expressing ill-considered, subjective opinions is not necessarily the worst sin beginning writers can commit; it might be a starting point from which they can move to more reasoned, less self-indulgent perspectives. Second, prohibiting students from using "I" is simply not an effective way of curbing student subjectivity, since one can offer poorly argued, ill-supported opinions just as easily without it. Third and most important, prohibiting the first person tends to hamper students' ability not only to take strong positions, but to differentiate their own positions from those of others, as we point out in Chapter 5. To be sure, writers can resort to various circumlocutions—"it will here be argued," "the evidence suggests," "the truth is"— and these may be useful for avoiding a monotonous series of "I believe" sentences. But except for avoiding such monotony, we see no good reason why "I" should be set aside in persuasive writing.

HOW THIS BOOK IS ORGANIZED

Because of its centrality, we have allowed the "they say / I say" format to dictate the structure of this book. So while Part 1 addresses the art of listening to others, Part 2 addresses how to offer one's own response. Part 1 opens with a chapter on "Starting with What Others Are Saying" that explains why it is generally advisable to begin a text by citing others rather than plunging directly into one's own views. Subsequent chapters take up the arts of summarizing and quoting what these others have to say. Part 2 begins with a chapter on different ways of responding, followed by chapters on marking the shift between what "they say" and what "I say," on introducing and answering objections, and on answering the all-important questions "so what?" and "who cares?" Part 3 offers strategies for "Tying It All Together," beginning with a chapter on connection and coherence; followed by a chapter on style, arguing that academic discourse is often perfectly compatible with the informal language that students use outside of school; and concluding with a chapter on the art of metacommentary, showing students how to guide the way readers understand their text. At the end of the book we include an appendix suggesting how the "they say / I say" model can improve classroom discussions, three model essays that we refer to in various chapters, and finally an Index of Templates.

WHAT THIS BOOK DOESN'T DO

There are some things that this book does not try to do. We do not, for instance, cover logical principles of argument such as syllogisms, warrants, logical fallacies, or the differences between inductive and deductive reasoning. Although such concepts can be useful, we believe most of us learn the ins and outs of argumentative writing not by studying logical principles in the abstract, but by plunging into actual discussions and debates, trying out different modes of response, and in this way getting a sense of what works to persuade different audiences and what doesn't. In our view, people learn more about arguing from hearing someone say, "You miss my point. What I'm saying is not _____, but _____," or, "I agree with you that _____, and would even add that _____," than they do from studying the differences between inductive and deductive reasoning. Such formulas give students an immediate sense of what it feels like to enter a public conversation in a way that studying abstract warrants and logical fallacies does not.

We also do not cover the various modes of writing like description, definition, narrative, and comparison/contrast. Nor do we cover the different conventions of writing in the disciplines. It is our belief, that the "they say / I say" pattern cuts across different disciplines and genres of writing, including creative writing. Although students must eventually master the specific writing conventions of their majors, we believe that there is no major or discipline that does not require writers to frame their own claims as a response to what others before them have said. Indeed, students who master the elemental moves prompted by the templates in this book should actually become *better* able to appreciate the differences between disciplines and genres.

ENGAGING THE VOICE OF THE OTHER

A major virtue of the "they say / I say'" model is that it returns writing to its social, conversational base. Although writing does require some degree of solitude, the "they say / I say" model shows students that they can best develop their arguments not just by looking inward, but also by looking outward, listening carefully to other views, and engaging the voice of the other. As a result, this approach to writing has an ethical dimension: it asks students not simply to keep proving and reasserting what they already believe, but to stretch what they believe by putting it up against the beliefs of our increasingly diverse, global society, to engage in the reciprocal exchange that characterizes true democracy.

Gerald Graff
Cathy Birkenstein

INTRODUCTION

Entering the Conversation

—◻—

THINK ABOUT AN activity that you do particularly well: cooking, playing the piano, shooting a basketball, even something as basic as driving a car. If you reflect on this activity, you'll realize that once you mastered it you no longer had to give much conscious thought to the various moves that go into doing it. Performing this activity, in other words, depends on your having learned a series of complicated moves—moves that may seem mysterious or difficult to those who haven't yet learned them.

The same applies to writing. Often without consciously realizing it, accomplished writers routinely rely on a stock of established moves that are crucial for communicating sophisticated ideas. What makes writers masters of their trade is not only their ability to express interesting thoughts, but their mastery of an inventory of basic moves that they probably picked up by reading a wide range of other accomplished writers. Less experienced writers, by contrast, are often unfamiliar with these basic moves, and unsure how to make them in their own writing. This book is intended as a short, user-friendly guide to the basic moves of persuasive writing.

One of our key premises is that these basic moves are so common that they can be represented in *templates* that you can use right away to structure and even generate your own writing. Perhaps the most distinctive feature of this book is its presentation of many such templates, designed to help you successfully enter not only the world of academic thinking and writing, but also the wider worlds of civic discourse and work.

Rather than focus solely on abstract principles of writing, then, this book offers model templates that help you to put those principles directly into practice. Working with these templates can give you an immediate sense of how to engage in the kinds of critical thinking you are required to do at the college level and in the vocational and public spheres beyond.

Some of these templates represent simple but crucial moves like those used to summarize some widely held belief.

▶ Many Americans assume that _____.

Others are more complicated.

▶ On the one hand, _____. On the other hand, _____.

▶ Author X contradicts herself. At the same time that she argues _____, she also implies _____.

▶ I agree that _____.

▶ This is not to say that _____.

It is true, of course, that critical thinking and writing go deeper than any set of linguistic formulas, requiring that you question assumptions, develop strong claims, offer supporting reasons and evidence, consider opposing arguments, and so on. But these deeper habits of thought cannot be put into practice unless you have a language for expressing them in clear, organized ways.

STATE YOUR OWN IDEAS AS A
RESPONSE TO OTHERS

The single most important template that we focus on in this book is the "they say _____, I say _____" formula that gives our book its title. If there is any one point that we hope you will take away from this book, it is the importance not only of expressing your ideas ("I say"), but of presenting those ideas as a *response to some other person or group* ("they say"). For us, the underlying structure of effective academic writing—and of responsible public discourse—resides not just in stating our own ideas, but in listening closely to others around us, summarizing their views in a way that they will recognize, and responding with our own ideas in kind. Broadly speaking, academic writing is argumentative writing, and we believe that to argue well you need to do more than assert your own ideas. You need to enter a conversation, using what others say (or might say) as a launching pad or sounding board for your own ideas. For this reason, one of the main pieces of advice in this book is to write the voices of others into your text.

In our view, then, the best academic writing has one underlying feature: it is deeply engaged in some way with other people's views. Too often, however, academic writing is taught as a process of saying "true" or "smart" things in a vacuum, as if it were possible to argue effectively without being in conversation *with* someone else. If you have been taught to write a traditional five-paragraph essay, for example, you have learned how to develop a thesis and support it with evidence. This is good advice as far as it goes, but it leaves out the important fact that in the real world we don't make arguments without being provoked. We make arguments because someone has said or done something (or perhaps *not* said or done something) and we need to respond: "I can't see why you like the Lakers so much"; "I agree: it was a great film"; "That argument is contradictory." If it weren't for other people and our need to challenge, agree with, or otherwise respond to them, there would be no reason to argue at all.

To make an impact as a writer, you need to do more than make statements that are logical, well supported, and consistent. You must also find a way of entering a conversation with others' views—with something "they say." In fact, if your own argument doesn't identify the "they say" that you're responding to, then it probably won't make sense. As Figure 1 suggests, *what* you are saying may be clear to your audience, but *why* you are saying it won't be. For it is what others are saying and thinking that motivates our writing and gives it a reason for being. It follows, then, as Figure 2 suggests, that your own argument—the "I say" moment of your text—should always be a response to the arguments of others.

Many writers make explicit "they say/I say" moves in their writing. One famous example is Martin Luther King Jr.'s "Let-

FIGURE 1

4

FIGURE 2

ter from Birmingham Jail," which consists almost entirely of King's eloquent responses to a public statement by eight clergymen deploring the civil rights protests he was leading. The letter—which was written in 1963, while King was in prison for leading a demonstration in Birmingham—is structured almost entirely around a framework of summary and response, in which King summarizes and then answers their criticisms. In one typical passage, King writes as follows.

> You deplore the demonstrations taking place in Birmingham. But your statement, I am sorry to say, fails to express a similar concern for the conditions that brought about the demonstrations.
>
> MARTIN LUTHER KING JR., "Letter from Birmingham Jail"

King goes on to agree with his critics that "It is unfortunate that demonstrations are taking place in Birmingham," yet he hastens to add that "it is even more unfortunate that the city's white power structure left the Negro community with no alternative." King's letter is so thoroughly conversational, in fact, that it could be rewritten in the form of a dialogue or play.

King's critics:
King's response:
Critics:
Response:

Clearly, King would not have written his famous letter were it not for his critics, whose views he treats not as objections to his already-formed arguments, but as the motivating source of those arguments, their central reason for being. He quotes not only what his critics have said ("Some have asked: 'Why didn't you give the new city administration time to act?'"), but also things they *might* have said ("One may well ask: 'How can you advocate breaking some laws and obeying others?'")—all to set the stage for what he himself wants to say.

A similar "they say/I say" exchange opens an essay about American patriotism by the social critic Katha Pollitt, who uses her own daughter's comment to represent the national fervor of post-9/11 patriotism that Pollitt goes on to oppose.

My daughter, who goes to Stuyvesant High School only blocks from the former World Trade Center, thinks we should fly the American flag out our window. Definitely not, I say: The flag stands for jingoism and vengeance and war.

KATHA POLLITT, "Put Out No Flags"

As Pollitt's example shows, the "they" you respond to in crafting an argument need not be a famous author, or even someone known to your audience. It can be a family member like Pollitt's daughter, or a friend or classmate who has made a provocative claim. It can even be something an individual or a group might say—or a side of yourself, something you once believed but no longer do, or something you partly believe but also doubt. The important thing is that the "they" (or "you" or "she") represent some wider group—in Pollitt's case, those who patriotically believe in flying the flag.

While King and Pollitt both identify the views they are responding to, in some cases those views, rather than being explicitly named, are left to the reader to infer. See, for instance, if you can identify the implied or unnamed "they say" that the following claim is responding to.

> I like to think I have a certain advantage as a teacher of literature because when I was growing up I disliked and feared books.
>
> GERALD GRAFF, "Disliking Books at an Early Age"

In case you haven't figured it out already, the phantom "they say" here is anyone who thinks that in order to be a good teacher of literature, one must have grown up liking and enjoying books.

As you can see from these examples, many writers use the "they say/I say" format to disagree with others, to challenge standard ways of thinking, and thus to stir up controversy. This point may come as a shock to you if you have always had the impression that in order to succeed academically you need to play it safe and avoid controversy in your writing, making statements that nobody can possibly disagree with. Though this view of writing may appear logical, it is actually a recipe for flat, lifeless writing, and for writing that fails to answer what we call the "so what?" and "who cares?" questions. "William Shakespeare wrote many famous plays and sonnets" may be a perfectly true statement, but precisely because nobody is likely to disagree with it, it goes without saying and thus would seem pointless if said.

WAYS OF RESPONDING

Just because much argumentative writing is driven by disagreement, it does not follow that *agreement* is ruled out. Although argumentation is often associated with conflict and opposition, the type of conversational "they say/I say" argument that we focus on in this book can be just as useful when you agree as when you disagree.

▸ She argues _____, and I agree because _____ .

▸ Her argument that _____ is supported by new research showing that _____ .

Nor do you always have to choose between either simply agreeing *or* disagreeing, since the "they say/I say" format also works to both agree and disagree at the same time.

▸ He claims that _____, and I have mixed feelings about it. On the one hand, I agree that _____. On the other hand, I still insist that _____ .

This last option—agreeing and disagreeing simultaneously—is one we especially recommend, since it allows you to avoid a simple yes or no response and present a more complicated argument, while containing that complication within a clear "on the one hand/on the other hand" framework.

While the templates we offer in this book can be used to structure your writing at the sentence level, they can also be expanded as needed to almost any length, as the following elaborated "they say/I say" template demonstrates.

In recent discussions of _____, a controversial issue has been whether _____. On the one hand, some argue that _____. From this perspective, _____. On the other hand, however, others argue that _____. In the words of one of this view's main proponents, "_____." According to this view, _____. In sum, then, the issue is whether _____ or _____.

My own view is that _____. Though I concede that _____, I still maintain that _____. For example, _____. Although some might object that _____, I reply that _____. The issue is important because _____.

If you go back over this template, you will see that it helps you make a host of challenging moves (each of which is taken up in forthcoming chapters in this book). First, the template helps you open your text by identifying an issue in some ongoing conversation or debate ("In recent discussions of _____, a controversial issue has been"), then to map some of the voices in this controversy (by using the "on the one hand/on the other hand" structure). The template also helps you to introduce a quotation ("In the words of"), to explain the quotation in your own words ("According to this view"), and—in a new paragraph—to state your own argument ("My own view is that"), to qualify your argument ("Though I concede that"), and then to support your argument with evidence ("For example"). In addition, the template helps you make one of the most crucial moves in argumentative writing, what we call "planting a naysayer in your text," in which you summarize and then answer a likely objection to your own central claim ("Although it might be objected that _____, I reply _____"). Finally, this template helps you shift between general, overarching claims ("In sum, then") and smaller-scale, supporting claims ("For example").

Again, none of us is born knowing these moves, especially when it comes to academic writing. Hence the need for this book.

DO TEMPLATES STIFLE CREATIVITY?

If you are like some of our students, your initial response to templates may be skepticism. At first, many of our students complain that using templates will take away their originality and creativity and make them all sound the same. "They'll turn us into writing robots," one of our students insisted. Another agreed, adding, "Hey, I'm a jazz musician. And we don't play by set forms. We create our own." "I'm in college now," another student asserted; "this is third-grade level stuff."

In our view, however, the templates in this book, far from being "third-grade level stuff," represent the stock in trade of sophisticated thinking and writing, and they often require a great deal of practice and instruction to use successfully. As for the belief that pre-established forms undermine creativity, we think it rests on a very limited vision of what creativity is all about. In our view, the above template and the others in this book will actually help your writing become *more* original and creative, not less. After all, even the most creative forms of expression depend on established patterns and structures. Most songwriters, for instance, rely on a time-honored verse-chorus-verse pattern, and few people would call Shakespeare uncreative because he didn't invent the sonnet or dramatic forms that he used to such dazzling effect. Even the most avant-garde, cutting-edge artists (like improvisational jazz musicians) need to master the basic forms that their work improvises on, departs from, and goes beyond, or else their work will come across as uneducated child's play. Ultimately, then, creativity and originality lie not in the avoidance of established forms, but in the imaginative use of them.

Furthermore, these templates do not dictate the *content* of what you say, which can be as original as you can make it, but only suggest a way of formatting *how* you say it. In addition, once you begin to feel comfortable with the templates in this book, you will be able to improvise creatively on them and invent new ones to fit new situations and purposes. In other words, the templates offered here are learning tools to get you started, not structures set in stone. Once you get used to using them, you can even dispense with them altogether, for the rhetorical moves they model will be at your fingertips in an unconscious, instinctive way.

But if you still need proof that writing templates do not stifle creativity, consider the following opening to an essay on the fast-food industry that we've included at the back of this book.

> If ever there were a newspaper headline custom-made for Jay Leno's monologue, this was it. Kids taking on McDonald's this week, suing the company for making them fat. Isn't that like middle-aged men suing Porsche for making them get speeding tickets? Whatever happened to personal responsibility?
>
> I tend to sympathize with these portly fast-food patrons, though. Maybe that's because I used to be one of them.
>
> DAVID ZINCZENKO, "Don't Blame the Eater"

Although Zinczenko relies on a version of the "they say/I say" formula, his writing is anything but dry, robotic, or uncreative. While Zinczenko does not explicitly use the words "they say" and "I say," the template still gives the passage its underlying structure: "*They say* that kids suing fast-food companies for making them fat is a joke; but *I say* such lawsuits are justified."

Putting in Your Oar

Though the immediate goal of this book is to help you become a better writer, at a deeper level it invites you to become a certain type of person: a critical, intellectual thinker who, instead of sitting passively on the sidelines, can participate in the debates and conversations of your world in an active and empowered way. Ultimately, this book invites you to become a critical thinker who can enter the types of conversations described eloquently by the philosopher Kenneth Burke in the following widely cited passage. Likening the world of intellectual exchange to a never-ending conversation at a party, Burke writes:

> You come late. When you arrive, others have long preceded you, and they are engaged in a heated discussion, a discussion too heated for them to pause and tell you exactly what it is about. . . . You listen for a while, until you decide that you have caught the tenor of the argument; then you put in your oar. Someone answers; you answer him; another comes to your defense; another aligns himself against you. . . . The hour grows late, you must depart. And you do depart, with the discussion still vigorously in progress.
>
> KENNETH BURKE, *The Philosophy of Literary Form*

What we like about this passage is its suggestion that stating an argument and "putting in your oar" can only be done in conversation with others; that we all enter the dynamic world of ideas not as isolated individuals, but as social beings deeply connected to others who have a stake in what we say.

This ability to enter complex, many-sided conversations has taken on a special urgency in today's diverse, post-9/11 world, where the future for all of us may depend on our ability to put ourselves in the shoes of those who think very differently from us. The central piece of advice in this book—that we listen carefully to others, including those who disagree with us, and then engage with them thoughtfully and respectfully—can help us see beyond our own pet beliefs, which may not be shared by everyone. The mere act of crafting a sentence that begins "Of course, someone might object that _____" may not seem like a way to change the world; but it does have the potential to jog us out of our comfort zones, to get us thinking critically about our own beliefs, and perhaps even to change our minds.

Exercises

1. Read the following paragraph from an essay by Emily Poe, a student at Furman University. Disregarding for the moment what Poe says, focus your attention on the phrases Poe uses to structure what she says (italicized here). Find a paragraph or two in some other text that makes similar moves, and underline the words the writer uses to structure what he or she says. Essays, newspaper editorials, and text-books might be good places to look.

The term "vegetarian" *tends to be synonymous with* "tree-hugger" *in many people's minds. They see* vegetarianism as a cult that brain-washes its followers into eliminating an essential part of their daily diets for an abstract goal of "animal welfare." *However,* few vegetarians choose their lifestyle just to follow the crowd. *On the contrary*, many of these supposedly brainwashed people are actually independent thinkers, concerned citizens, and compassionate human beings. *For the truth is* that there are many very good reasons for giving up meat. Perhaps the best reasons are to improve the environment, to encourage humane treatment of livestock, or to enhance one's own health. *In this essay, then, closely examining* a vegetarian diet as compared to a meat-eater's diet *will show that* vegetarianism is clearly the better option for sustaining the Earth and all its inhabitants.

2. Write a short essay in which you first summarize our rationale for the templates in this book and then articulate your own position in response. If you want, you can use the template below to organize your paragraphs, expanding and modifying it as necessary to fit what you want to say. If you choose not to use the template, explain why you believe your own writing method is preferable.

   ▶ In the Introduction to "*They Say/I Say*": *The Moves That Matter in Academic Writing,* Gerald Graff and Cathy Birkenstein provide templates designed to _____. Specifically, Graff and Birkenstein argue that the types of writing templates they offer _____. As the authors themselves put it, "_____." Although some people believe _____, Graff and Birkenstein insist that _____. In sum, then, their view is that _____.

   I agree/disagree/have mixed feelings. In my view, the types of templates that the authors recommend _____. For instance, _____. In addition, _____. Some might object, of course, on the grounds that _____. Yet I would argue that _____. Overall, then, I believe _____—an important point to make given _____.

1

"THEY SAY"

—▱—

ONE

"THEY SAY"

Starting with What Others Are Saying

—◻—

NOT LONG AGO we attended a talk at an academic conference where the speaker's central claim seemed to be that a certain sociologist—call him Dr. X—had done very good work in a number of areas of the discipline. The speaker proceeded to illustrate his thesis by referring extensively and in great detail to various books and articles by Dr. X and by quoting long passages from them. The speaker was obviously both learned and impassioned, but as we listened to his talk we found ourselves somewhat puzzled: the argument—that Dr. X's work was very important—was clear enough, but why did the speaker need to make it in the first place? Did anyone dispute it? Were there commentators in the field who had argued against X's work or challenged its value? Was the speaker's interpretation of what X had done somehow novel or revolutionary? Since he gave no hint of an answer to any of these questions, we could only wonder why he was going on and on about X. It was only after the speaker finished and took questions from the audience that we got a clue: in response to one questioner, he referred to several critics who had vigorously questioned Dr. X's ideas and convinced many sociologists that Dr. X's work was unsound.

This little story illustrates an important lesson: that to give writing the most important thing of all—namely, a point—a writer needs to indicate clearly not only his or her thesis, but also what larger conversation that thesis is responding to. Because our speaker failed to mention what others had said about Dr. X's work, he left his audience unsure about why he felt the need to say what he was saying. Perhaps the point was clear to other sociologists in the audience who were more familiar with the debates over Dr. X's work than we were. But even they, we bet, would have understood the speaker's point better if he'd sketched in some of the larger conversation his own claims were a part of and reminded the audience about what "they say."

This story also illustrates an important lesson about the *order* in which things are said: to keep an audience engaged, a writer needs to explain what he or she is responding to either before offering that response or, at least, very early in the discussion. Delaying this explanation for more than one or two paragraphs in a very short essay, three or four pages in a longer one, or more than ten or so pages in a book-length text reverses the natural order in which readers process material—and in which writers think and develop ideas. After all, it seems very unlikely that our conference speaker first developed his defense of Dr. X and only later came across Dr. X's critics. As someone knowledgeable in his field, the speaker surely encountered the criticisms first and only then was compelled to respond and, as he saw it, set the record straight.

Therefore, when it comes to constructing an argument (whether orally or in writing), we offer you the following advice: remember that you are entering a conversation and therefore need to start with "what others are saying," as the title of this chapter recommends, and then introduce your own ideas as a response. Specifically, we suggest that you summarize what "they say" as soon as you can in your text, and remind readers of it at strategic points as your text unfolds. Though it's true that not all texts follow this practice, we think it's important for all writers to master it before they depart from it.

This is not to say that you must start with a detailed list of everyone who has written on your subject before you offer your own ideas. Had our conference speaker gone to the opposite extreme and spent most of his talk summarizing Dr. X's critics with no hint of what he himself had to say, the audience probably would have had the same frustrated "why-is-he-going-on-like this?" reaction. What we suggest, then, is that as soon as possible you state your own position and the one it's responding to *together*, and that you think of the two as a unit. It is generally best to summarize the ideas you're responding to briefly, at the start of your text, and to delay detailed elaboration until later. The point is to give your readers a quick preview of what is motivating your argument, not to drown them in details this early.

Starting with a summary of others' views may seem to contradict the common advice that writers lead with their own thesis or central claim. Although we agree that you shouldn't keep readers in suspense too long about your central argument, we also believe that you need to present that argument as part of some larger conversation, to indicate something about the arguments of others that you are supporting, opposing, amending, complicating, or qualifying. One added benefit of summarizing others' views as soon as you can: those others do some of the work of framing and clarifying the issue you're writing about.

Consider, for example, how George Orwell starts his famous essay "Politics and the English Language" with what others are saying.

> Most people who bother with the matter at all would admit that the English language is in a bad way, but it is generally assumed that we cannot by conscious action do anything about it. Our civilization is decadent and our language—so the argument runs—must inevitably share in the general collapse. . . .
>
> [But] the process is reversible. Modern English . . . is full of bad habits . . . which can be avoided if one is willing to take the necessary trouble.
>
> GEORGE ORWELL, "Politics and the English Language"

Orwell is basically saying, "Most people assume that we cannot do anything about the bad state of the English language. But I say we can."

Of course, there are many other powerful ways to begin. Instead of opening with someone else's views, you could start with an illustrative quotation, a revealing fact or statistic, or—as we do in this chapter—a relevant anecdote. If you choose one of these formats, however, be sure that it in some way illustrates the view you're addressing or leads you to that view directly, with a minimum of steps.

In opening this chapter, for example, we devote the first paragraph to an anecdote about the conference speaker and then move quickly at the start of the second paragraph to the anecdote's "important lesson" regarding what speakers should and shouldn't do. In the following opening, from a 2004 opinion piece in the *New York Times Book Review*, Christina Nehring also moves quickly from an anecdote illustrating something she dislikes to her own claim—that book lovers think too highly of themselves.

> "I'm a reader!" announced the yellow button. "How about you?" I looked at its bearer, a strapping young guy stalking my town's Festi-val of Books. "I'll bet you're a reader," he volunteered, as though we were two geniuses well met. "No," I replied. "Absolutely not," I wanted to yell, and fling my Barnes & Noble bag at his feet. Instead, I mumbled something apologetic and melted into the crowd.
>
> There's a new piety in the air: the self congratulation of book lovers.
>
> CHRISTINA NEHRING, "Books Make You a Boring Person"

Nehring's anecdote is really a kind of "they say": book lovers keep telling themselves how great they are.

TEMPLATES FOR INTRODUCING WHAT "THEY SAY"

There are lots of conventional moves for introducing what others are saying. Here are some standard templates that we would have recommended to our conference speaker.

▶ A number of sociologists have recently suggested that X's work has several fundamental problems.

▶ It has become common today to dismiss X's contribution to the field of sociology.

▶ In their recent work, Y and Z have offered harsh critiques of Dr. X for _____.

TEMPLATES FOR INTRODUCING "STANDARD VIEWS"

The following templates can help you make what we call the "standard view" move, in which you introduce a view that has become so widely accepted that by now it is essentially the conventional way of thinking about a topic.

▸ Americans today tend to believe that _____.

▸ Conventional wisdom has it that _____.

▸ Common sense seems to dictate that _____.

▸ The standard way of thinking about topic X has it that _____.

▸ It is often said that _____.

▸ My whole life I have heard it said that _____.

▸ You would think that _____.

▸ Many people assume that _____.

These templates are popular because they provide a quick and efficient way to perform one of the most common moves that writers make: challenging widely accepted beliefs, placing them on the examining table and analyzing their strengths and weaknesses.

TEMPLATES FOR MAKING WHAT "THEY SAY" SOMETHING *YOU* SAY

Another way to introduce the views you're responding to is to present them as your own.

► I've always believed that _____.

► When I was a child, I used to think that _____.

► Although I should know better by now, I cannot help thinking that _____.

► At the same time that I believe _____, I also believe _____.

TEMPLATES FOR INTRODUCING SOMETHING IMPLIED OR ASSUMED

Another sophisticated move a writer can make is to summarize a point that is not directly stated in what "they say" but is implied or assumed.

► Although none of them have ever said so directly, my teachers have often given me the impression that _____.

► One implication of X's treatment of _____ is that _____.

► Although X does not say so directly, she apparently assumes that _____.

► While they rarely admit as much, _____ often take for granted that _____.

These are templates that can really help you to think critically—to look beyond what others say explicitly and to consider their unstated assumptions, as well as the implications of their views.

TEMPLATES FOR INTRODUCING
AN ONGOING DEBATE

Sometimes you'll want to open by summarizing a debate that presents two or more views. This kind of opening demonstrates your awareness that there are many ways to look at your subject, the clear mark of someone deeply familiar with the subject and therefore likely to be a reliable, trustworthy guide. Furthermore, opening with a summary of a debate can help you to frame and explore the issue you are writing about before declaring your own view. In this way, you can use the writing process itself to help you discover where you stand instead of having to take a position before you are ready to do so.

Here is a basic template for opening with a debate.

▶ In discussions of X, one controversial issue has been _____. On the one hand, _____ argues _____. On the other hand, _____ contends _____. Others even maintain _____. My own view is _____.

The cognitive scientist Mark Aronoff uses this kind of template in an essay on the workings of the human brain.

> Theories of how the mind/brain works have been dominated for centuries by two opposing views. One, rationalism, sees the human mind as coming into this world more or less fully formed—preprogrammed, in modern terms. The other, empiricism, sees the mind of the newborn as largely unstructured, a blank slate.
> MARK ARONOFF, "Washington Slept Here"

Another way to open with a debate involves starting with a proposition many people agree with in order to highlight the point(s) on which they ultimately disagree.

▸ When it comes to the topic of _____, most of us will readily agree that _____. Where this agreement usually ends, however, is on the question of _____. Whereas some are convinced that _____, others maintain that

_____.

The political writer Thomas Frank, writing on the 2004 presidential election, uses a variation on this sophisticated move.

> That we are a nation divided is an almost universal lament of this bitter election year. However, the exact property that divides us—elemental though it is said to be—remains a matter of some controversy.
>
> THOMAS FRANK, "American Psyche"

While templates like these help you introduce what others are saying at the start of your text, Chapters 2 and 3 explore the arts of summarizing and quoting in more detail.

KEEP WHAT "THEY SAY" IN VIEW

We can't urge you too strongly to keep in mind what "they say" as you move through the rest of your text. After summarizing the ideas you are responding to at the outset, it's very important to continue to keep those ideas in view. Readers won't be able to follow your unfolding response, much less any complications you may offer, unless you keep reminding them what claims you are responding to.

In other words, even when presenting your own claims, you should keep returning to the motivating "they say." The longer and more complicated your text, the greater the chance that readers will forget what ideas originally motivated it—no matter how clearly you lay them out at the outset. At strategic moments throughout your text, we recommend that you include what we call "return sentences." Here is an example.

▸ In conclusion, then, as I suggested earlier, defenders of
  _____ can't have it both ways. Their assertion that _____
  is contradicted by their claim that _____ .

We ourselves use such return sentences at every opportunity in this book to remind you of the view of writing that our book challenges—that good writing means making true or smart or logical statements about a given subject with little or no reference to what others say about it.

By reminding readers of the ideas you're responding to, return sentences ensure that your text maintains a sense of mission and urgency from start to finish. In short, they help ensure that your argument is a genuine response to others' views rather than just a set of observations about a given subject. The difference is huge. To be responsive to others and the conversation you're entering, you need not only to start with what others are saying, but also to continue keeping it in the reader's view.

Exercises

1. The following claims all provide an "I say." See if you can supply a plausible "they say" for each one. It may help to

use one of the Templates for Introducing What "They Say" (p. 21).

- a. Our experiments suggest that there are dangerous levels of Chemical X in the Ohio groundwater.
- b. My own view is that this novel has certain flaws.
- c. Football is so boring.
- d. Male students often dominate class discussions.
- e. In my view the film is really about the problems of romantic relationships.
- f. I'm afraid that templates like the ones in this book will stifle my creativity.

2. Below is a template that we derived from the opening of David Zinczenko's "Don't Blame the Eater" (p. 139). Use the template to structure a passage on a topic of your own choosing. Your first step here should be to find an idea that you support that others not only disagree with, but actually find laughable (or, as Zinczenko puts it, worthy of a Jay Leno monologue). You might write about one of the topics listed in the previous exercise (the environment, sports, gender relations, the meaning of a book or movie) or any other topic that interests you.

  ▸ If ever there was an idea custom-made for a Jay Leno monologue, this was it: _____. Isn't that like _____? Whatever happened to _____?

    I happen to sympathize with _____, though, perhaps because _____.

TWO

"HER POINT IS"

The Art of Summarizing

—▣—

IF IT IS TRUE, as we claim in this book, that to argue persuasively you need to be in dialogue with others, then summarizing others' arguments is central to your arsenal of basic moves. Because writers who make strong claims need to map their claims relative to those of other people, it is important to know how to summarize effectively what those other people say. (We're using the word "summarizing" here to refer to any information from others that you present in your own words, including that which you paraphrase.)

Many writers shy away from summarizing—perhaps because they don't want to take the trouble to go back to the text in question and wrestle with what it says, or because they fear that devoting too much time to other people's ideas will take away from their own. When assigned to write a response to an article, such writers might offer their own views on the article's *topic* while hardly mentioning what the article itself argues or says. At the opposite extreme are those who do nothing *but* summarize. Lacking confidence, perhaps, in their own ideas, these writers so overload their texts with summaries of others' ideas that their own voice gets lost. And since these summaries are not animated by the writers' own interests, they often read like mere lists of things that X thinks or Y says—with no clear focus.

As a general rule, a good summary requires balancing what the original author is saying with the writer's own focus. Generally speaking, a summary must at once be true to what the original author says while at the same time emphasizing those aspects of what the author says that interest you, the writer. Striking this delicate balance can be tricky, since it means facing two ways at once: both outward (toward the author being summarized) and inward (toward yourself). Ultimately, it means being respectful of others while simultaneously structuring how you summarize them in light of your own text's central claim.

ON THE ONE HAND,
PUT YOURSELF IN *THEIR* SHOES

To write a really good summary, you must be able to suspend your own beliefs for a time and put yourself in the shoes of someone else. This means playing what the writing theorist Peter Elbow calls the "believing game," in which you try to inhabit the worldview of those whose conversation you are joining—and whom you are perhaps even disagreeing with—and try to see their argument from their perspective. This ability to temporarily suspend one's own convictions is a hallmark of good actors, who must convincingly "become" characters who in real life they may actually detest. As a writer, when you play the believing game really well, readers should not be able to tell whether you agree or disagree with the ideas you are summarizing.

If, as a writer, you cannot or will not suspend your own beliefs in this way, you are likely to produce summaries that are so obviously biased that they undermine your credibility with readers. Consider the following summary.

> In his article "Don't Blame the Eater," David Zinczenko accuses the fast-food companies of an evil conspiracy to make people fat. I disagree because these companies have to make money.

If you review what Zinczenko actually says (pp. 139–41), you should immediately see that this summary amounts to an unfair distortion. While Zinczenko does argue that the practices of the fast-food industry have the *effect* of making people fat, he never goes so far as to suggest that the fast-food industry conspires to do so with deliberately evil intent.

Another tell-tale sign of this writer's failure to give Zinczenko a fair hearing is the hasty way he abandons the summary after only one sentence and rushes on to his own response. So eager is this writer to disagree that he not only caricatures what Zinczenko says but also gives the article a hasty, superficial reading. Granted, there are many writing situations in which, because of matters of proportion, a one- or two-sentence summary is precisely what you want. Indeed, as writing professor Karen Lunsford (whose own research focuses on argument theory) points out, it is standard in the natural and social sciences to summarize the work of others quickly, in one pithy sentence or phrase, as in the following example.

> Several studies (Crackle, 1992; Pop, 2001; Snap, 1987) suggest that these policies are harmless; moreover, other studies (Dick, 2002; Harry, 2003; Tom, 1987) argue that they even have benefits.

But if your assignment is to respond in writing to a single author like Zinczenko, then you will need to tell your readers enough about his or her argument so they can assess its merits on their own, independent of you.

When a writer fails to play the believing game, he or she often falls prey to what we call "the closest cliché syndrome," in which what gets summarized is not the view the author in question has actually expressed, but a familiar cliché that the writer *mistakes* for the author's view (sometimes because the writer believes it and mistakenly assumes the author must too). So, for example, Martin Luther King Jr.'s passionate defense of civil disobedience in "Letter from Birmingham Jail" gets summarized not as the defense of political protest that it actually is, but as a plea for everyone to "just get along." Similarly, Zinczenko's critique of the fast-food industry might get summarized as a call for over-weight people to take responsibility for their weight.

Whenever you enter into a conversation with others in your writing, then, it is extremely important that you go back to what those others have said, that you study it very closely, and that you not collapse it to something you already have heard or know. Writers who fail to do this end up essentially conversing with themselves—with imaginary others who are really only the products of their own biases and preconceptions.

ON THE OTHER HAND, KNOW WHERE *YOU* ARE GOING

Even as writing an effective summary requires you to temporarily adopt the worldviews of others, it does not mean ignoring your own views altogether. Paradoxically, at the same time that summarizing another text requires you to represent fairly what it says, it also requires that your own response exert a quiet influence. A good summary, in other words, has a focus or spin that allows the summary to fit with your own overall agenda while still being true to the text you are summarizing.

If you read the essay by David Zinczenko (pp. 139–41), you should be able to see that an essay on the fast-food industry in general will call for a very different summary than will an essay on parenting, corporate regulation, or warning labels. If you want to address all three, fine; but in that case you'll need to subordinate these three issues to one of Zinczenko's general claims and then make sure this general claim directly sets up your own argument.

For example, suppose you want to argue that it is parents, not fast-food companies, who are to blame for children's obesity. To set up this argument, you will probably want to compose a summary that highlights what Zinczenko says about the fast-food industry and parents. Consider this sample.

> In his article "Don't Blame the Eater," David Zinczenko argues that today's fast-food chains fill the nutritional void in children's lives left by their overtaxed working parents. With many parents working long hours and unable to supervise what their children eat, Zinczenko claims, children today regularly turn to low-cost, calorie-laden foods that the fast-food chains are all too eager to supply. When he himself was a young boy, for instance, and his single mother was away at work, he ate at Taco Bell, McDonald's, and other chains on a regular basis, and ended up overweight. Zinczenko's hope is that with the new spate of lawsuits against the food industry, other children with working parents will have healthier choices available to them, and that they will not, like him, become obese.
>
> In my view, however, it is the parents, and not the food chains, who are responsible for their children's obesity. While it is true that many of today's parents work long hours, there are still several things that parents can do to guarantee that their children eat healthy foods. . .

This summary succeeds not only because it provides one big claim under which several of Zinczenko's points neatly fit ("today's fast-food chains fill the nutritional void in children's lives left by their overtaxed working parents"), but also because this big claim points toward the second paragraph: the writer's own thesis about parental responsibility. A less astute, less focused summary would merely include Zinczenko's indictment of the fast-food industry and ignore what he says about parents.

This advice—to summarize each author in terms of the specific issue your own argument focuses on—may seem painfully obvious. But writers who aren't attuned to these issues often summarize a given author on one issue even though their text actually focuses on another. To avoid this problem, you need to make sure that your "they say" and "I say" are well matched. In fact, aligning what they say with what you say is a good thing to work on when revising what you've written.

Often writers who summarize without regard to their own interests fall prey to what might be called "list summaries," summaries that simply inventory the original author's various points but fail to focus those points around any larger overall claim. If you've ever heard a talk in which the points were connected only by words like "and then," "also," and "in addition," you know how such lists can put listeners to sleep—as shown in Figure 3. A typical list summary sounds like this.

> The author says many different things about his subject. *First* he says. . . . *Then* he makes the point that. . . . *In addition* he says. . . . *And then* he writes. . . . *Also* he shows that. . . . *And then* he says. . . .

It may be boring list summaries like this that give summaries in general a bad name and even prompt some instructors to discourage their students from summarizing at all.

THE EFFECT OF A TYPICAL LIST SUMMARY

FIGURE 3

In conclusion, writing a good summary means not just representing an author's view accurately, but doing so in a way that fits your own composition's larger agenda. On the one hand, it means playing Peter Elbow's believing game and doing justice to the source; if the summary ignores or misrepresents the source, its bias and unfairness will show. On the other hand, even as it does justice to the source, a summary has to have a slant or spin that prepares the way for your own claims. Once a summary enters your text, you should think of it as joint property—reflecting both the source you are summarizing and you yourself.

SUMMARIZING SATIRICALLY

Thus far in this chapter we have argued that, as a general rule, good summaries require a balance between what someone else has said and your own interests as a writer. Now, however, we want to address one exception to this rule: the satiric summary, in which a writer deliberately gives his or her own spin to someone else's argument in order to reveal a glaring shortcoming in it. Despite our previous comments that well-crafted summaries generally strike a balance between heeding what someone else has said and your own, independent interests, the satiric mode can at times be a very effective form of critique because it lets the summarized argument condemn itself without overt editorializing by you, the writer. If you've ever watched *The Daily Show*, you'll recall that it basically summarizes silly things political leaders have said or done, letting their words or actions undermine themselves.

Consider another example. In late September 2001, President Bush in a speech to Congress urged the nation's "continued participation and confidence in the American economy" as a means of recovering from the terrorist attacks of 9/11. The journalist Allan Sloan made fun of this proposal simply by summarizing it, observing that the president had equated "patriotism with shopping. Maxing out your credit cards at the mall wasn't self indulgence, it was a way to get back at Osama bin Laden." Sloan's summary leaves no doubt where he stands— he considers Bush's proposal ridiculous, or at least too simple.

MAKE VERBS FIT THE ACTION

In introducing summaries, try to avoid bland formulas like "he talks about," "she says," or "they believe." Though language like this is sometimes serviceable enough, it often fails to capture accurately what the person has said. In some cases, "he says" may even drain the passion out of the ideas you're summarizing.

We suspect that the habit of ignoring the action in what we summarize stems from the mistaken belief we mentioned earlier that writing is about playing it safe and not making waves, a matter of piling up truths and bits of knowledge rather than a dynamic process of doing things to and with other people. People who wouldn't hesitate to *say* "X totally misrepresented" something when chatting with friends will in their writing often opt for far tamer and even less accurate phrases like "X said."

But the authors whom we care enough to write about never simply "say" or "discuss" things; they "urge," "emphasize," and "insist on" them. David Zinczenko, for example, doesn't just *say* that fast-food companies contribute to obesity; he *complains* or *protests* that they do; he *challenges, chastises,* and *indicts* those companies. The Declaration of Independence doesn't just *talk about* the treatment of the colonies by the British; it *protests against* it. To do justice to the authors you cite, we recommend that when summarizing—or even when introducing a quotation—you use vivid and precise signal verbs as often as possible. Though "he says" or "she believes" will sometimes be the most appropriate language for the occasion, your text will often be more accurate and lively if you tailor your verbs to suit the precise actions you're describing.

TEMPLATES FOR INTRODUCING SUMMARIES AND QUOTATIONS

▶ She demonstrates that _____.

▶ In fact, they celebrate the fact that _____.

▶ _____, he admits.

VERBS FOR INTRODUCING SUMMARIES AND QUOTATIONS

VERBS FOR MAKING A CLAIM

argue	insist
assert	observe
believe	remind us
claim	report
emphasize	suggest

VERBS FOR EXPRESSING AGREEMENT

acknowledge	endorse
admire	extol
agree	praise
concur	reaffirm
corroborate	support
do not deny	verify

VERBS FOR QUESTIONING OR DISAGREEING

complain	disavow
complicate	question
contend	refute
contradict	reject
deny	renounce
deplore the tendency to	repudiate

VERBS FOR MAKING RECOMMENDATIONS

advocate	implore
call for	plead
demand	recommend
encourage	urge
exhort	warn

Exercises

1. To get a feel for Peter Elbow's "believing game," write a summary of some belief that you strongly disagree with. Then write a summary of the position that you actually hold on this topic. Give both summaries to a classmate or two, and see if they can tell which position you endorse. If you've succeeded, they won't be able to tell.

2. Write two different summaries of David Zinczenko's "Don't Blame the Eater" (pp. 139–41). Write the first one for an essay arguing that, contrary to what Zinczenko claims, there *are* inexpensive and convenient alternatives to fast-food restaurants. Write the second for an essay that agrees with Zinczenko in blaming fast-food companies for youthful obesity, but questions his view that bringing lawsuits against those companies is a legitimate response to the problem. Compare your two summaries: though they are of the same article, they should look very different.

THREE

"As He Himself Puts It"

The Art of Quoting

———⌐◻⌐———

A KEY PREMISE of this book is that to launch an effective argument you need to write the arguments of others into your text. One of the best ways to do this is by not only summarizing what "they say," as suggested in Chapter 2, but by quoting their exact words. Quoting someone else's words gives a tremendous amount of credibility to your summary and helps ensure that it is fair and accurate. In a sense, then, quotations function as a kind of evidence, saying to readers: "Look, I'm not just making this up. She makes this claim and here it is in her exact words."

Yet many writers make a host of mistakes when it comes to quoting, not the least of which is the failure to quote enough in the first place, if at all. Some writers quote too little— perhaps because they don't want to bother going back to the original text and looking up the author's exact words, or because they think they can reconstruct the author's ideas from memory. At the opposite extreme are writers who so overquote that they end up with texts that are short on commentary of their own—maybe because they lack confidence in their ability to comment on the quotations, or because they don't fully understand them and therefore have trouble explaining what they mean.

But the main problem with quotation arises when writers assume that quotations speak for themselves. Because the meaning of a quotation is obvious to *them*, many writers assume that this meaning will also be obvious to their readers, when often it is not. Writers who make this mistake think that their job is done when they've chosen a quotation and inserted it into their text. They draft an essay, slap in a few quotations, and whammo, they're done.

Such writers fail to see that quoting means more than simply enclosing what "they say" in quotation marks. In a way, quotations are orphans: words that have been taken from their original contexts and that need to be integrated into their new textual surroundings. This chapter offers two key ways to produce this sort of integration: (1) by choosing quotations wisely, with an eye to how well they support a particular part of your text, and (2) by surrounding every major quotation with a frame explaining whose words they are, what the quotation means, and how the quotation relates to your text. The point we want to emphasize is that quoting what "they say" must always be connected with what *you* say.

Quote Relevant Passages

Before you can select appropriate quotations, you need to have a sense of what you want to do with them—that is, how they will support your text at the particular point where you insert them. Be careful not to select quotations just for the sake of demonstrating that you've read the author's work; you need to make sure they are relevant to your work.

However, finding relevant quotations is not always easy. In fact, sometimes quotations that were initially relevant to your overall argument, or to a key point in it, become less so as your text changes during the process of writing and revising. Given the evolving and messy nature of writing, you may sometimes think that you've found the perfect quotation to support your argument, only to discover later on, as your text develops, that your focus has changed and the quotation no longer works. It can be somewhat misleading, then, to speak of finding your thesis and finding relevant quotations as two separate steps, one coming after the other. When you're deeply engaged in the writing and revising process, there is usually a great deal of back-and-forth between your argument and any quotations you select.

FRAME EVERY QUOTATION

Finding relevant quotations is only part of your job; you also need to present them in a way that makes their relevance and meaning clear to your readers. Since quotations do not speak for themselves, you need to build a frame around them in which you do that speaking for them.

Quotations that are inserted into a text without such a frame are sometimes called "dangling" quotations for the way they're left dangling without any explanation. One graduate teaching assistant we work with, Steve Benton, calls these "hit-and-run" quotations, likening them to car accidents in which the driver speeds away and avoids taking responsibility for the dent in your fender or the smashed taillights (as in Figure 4).

On the following page is a typical hit-and-run quotation by a writer responding to an essay by the feminist philosopher Susan Bordo (reprinted on pp. 149–61).

DON'T BE A HIT-AND-RUN QUOTER.

FIGURE 4

Susan Bordo writes about women and dieting. "Fiji is just one example. Until television was introduced in 1995, the islands had no reported cases of eating disorders. In 1998, three years after programs from the United States and Britain began broadcasting there, 62 percent of the girls surveyed reported dieting."

I think Bordo is right. Another point Bordo makes is that. . . .

This writer fails to introduce the quotation adequately or explain why he finds it worth quoting. Besides neglecting to say who Bordo is or even that the quoted words are hers, the writer does not explain how her words connect with anything he is saying. He simply drops the quotation in his haste to zoom on to another point.

To adequately frame a quotation, you need to insert it into what we like to call a "quotation sandwich," with the statement introducing it serving as the top slice of bread and the explanation following it serving as the bottom slice. The introductory or lead-in claims should explain who is speaking and set up what the quotation says; the follow-up statements should explain why you consider the quotation to be important and what you take it to say.

TEMPLATES FOR INTRODUCING QUOTATIONS

▸ X states, "_____."

▸ As the prominent philosopher X puts it, "_____."

▸ According to X, "_____."

▸ X himself writes, "_____."

▸ In her book, _____, X maintains that "_____."

▸ Writing in the journal *Commentary*, X complains that "_____."

▸ In X's view, "_____."

▸ X agrees when she writes, "_____."

▸ X disagrees when he writes, "_____."

▸ X complicates matters further when she writes, "_____."

When adding such introductory phrases, be sure to use language that accurately reflects the spirit of the quoted passage. It is quite serviceable to write "Bordo states" or "asserts" in introducing the quotation about Fiji. But given the fact that Bordo is clearly alarmed by the effect of the extension of the media's reach to Fiji, it is far more accurate to use language that reflects her alarm: "Bordo is alarmed that" or "is disturbed by" or "complains." (See Chapter 2 for a list of verbs for introducing what others say.)

TEMPLATES FOR EXPLAINING QUOTATIONS

▸ Basically, X is saying _____ .

▸ In other words, X believes _____ .

▸ In making this comment, X argues that _____ .

▸ X is insisting that _____ .

▸ X's point is that _____ .

▸ The essence of X's argument is that _____ .

We suggest getting in the habit of following every major quotation with explanatory sentences structured by templates like these. Consider, for example, how the above passage on Bordo might be revised using some of these moves.

The feminist philosopher Susan Bordo deplores the hold that the Western obsession with dieting has on women. Her basic argument is that increasing numbers of women across the globe are being led to see themselves as fat and in need of a diet. Citing the island of Fiji as a case in point, Bordo notes that "until television was introduced in 1995, the islands had no reported cases of eating disorders. In 1998, three years after programs from the United States and Britain began broadcasting there, 62 percent of the girls surveyed reported dieting" (149–50). Bordo's point is that the West's obsession with dieting is spreading even to remote places across the globe. Ultimately, Bordo complains, the culture of dieting will find you, regardless of where you live.

Bordo's observations ring true to me because a friend of mine from a remote area in China speaks of the cult of dieting among young women there. . . .

This framing of the quotation not only helps to better integrate Bordo's words into the writer's text, but also serves to demonstrate the writer's interpretation of what Bordo is saying. While "the feminist philosopher" and "Bordo notes" provide basic information that readers need to know, the sentences that follow the quotation build a bridge between Bordo's words and those of the writer. Just as important, these sentences explain what Bordo is saying in the writer's own words—and thereby make clear that the quotation is being used purposefully to set up the writer's own argument and has not been stuck in just for padding or merely to have a citation.

BLEND THE AUTHOR'S WORDS WITH YOUR OWN

The above framing material works well because it accurately represents Bordo's words while at the same time giving those words the writer's own spin. Instead of simply repeating Bordo word for word, the follow-up sentences echo just enough of her text while still moving the discussion in the writer's own direction.

Notice how the passage refers several times to the key concept of dieting, and how it echoes Bordo's references to "television" and to U.S. and British "broadcasting" by referring to "culture," which is further specified as that of "the West."

Despite some repetition, this passage avoids merely restating what Bordo says. Her reference to 62 percent of Fijian girls dieting is no longer an inert statistic (as it was in the flawed passage presented earlier), but a quantitative example of how "the West's obsession with dieting is spreading . . . across the globe." In effect, the framing creates a kind of hybrid text, a mix of Bordo's words and those of the writer.

But is it possible to overexplain a quotation? And how do you know when you've explained a quotation thoroughly enough? After all, not all quotations require the same amount of explanatory framing, and there are no hard-and-fast rules for knowing how much explanation any quotation needs. As a general rule, the most explanatory framing is needed for quotations that may be hard for readers to process: quotations that are long and complex, that are filled with details or jargon, or that contain hidden complexities.

And yet, though the particular situation usually dictates when and how much to explain a quotation, we will still offer one piece of advice: when in doubt, go for it. It is better to risk being overly explicit about what you take a quotation to mean than to leave the quotation dangling and your readers in doubt. Indeed, we encourage you to provide such explanatory framing even when writing to an audience that you know to be familiar with the author being quoted and able to interpret your quotations on their own. Even in such cases readers need to see how *you* interpret the quotation, since words—especially those of controversial figures—can be interpreted in various ways and used to support different, sometimes opposing, agendas. Your readers need to see what you make of the material you've quoted, if only to be sure that your reading of the material and theirs is on the same page.

How *Not* to Introduce Quotations

We want to conclude this chapter by surveying some ways *not* to introduce quotations. Although some writers do so, you should not introduce quotations by saying something like "X asserts an idea that" or "A quote by X says." Introductory phrases like these are both redundant and misleading. In the first example, you could write either "X asserts that" or "X's idea is that," rather than redundantly combining the two. The second example misleads readers, since it is the writer who is doing the quoting, not X (as "a quote by X" implies).

The templates in this book will help you avoid such mistakes. And once you have mastered such templates you probably won't even have to think about them—and will be free to focus on the important, challenging ideas that the templates frame.

Exercises

1. Find a text that quotes someone's exact words as evidence of something that "they say." How has the writer integrated the quotation into his or her own text? How has he or she introduced it, and what if anything has the writer said to explain it and tie it to his or her own text? Based on what you've read in this chapter, are there any changes you would suggest?

2. Look at an essay or a report that you have written for one of your classes. Have you quoted any sources? If so, how have you integrated the quotation into your own text? How have you introduced it? Explained what it means? Indicated how it relates to *your* text? If you haven't done all these things, revise your text to do so, perhaps using the Templates for Introducing Quotations (p. 43) and Explaining Quotations (p. 44). If you've not written anything with quotations, try revising some academic text you've written to do so.

2

"I SAY"

FOUR

"YES / NO / OKAY, BUT"

Three Ways to Respond

———

OUR FIRST THREE chapters discuss the "they say" stage of writing, in which you devote your attention to the views of some other person or group. In this chapter we move to the "I say" stage, in which you offer your own argument as a response to what "they" have said.

There are a great many ways to respond, but this chapter concentrates on the three most common and recognizable ways: agreeing, disagreeing, or some combination of both. Although each way of responding is open to endless variation, we focus on these three because readers come to any text needing fairly quickly to learn where the writer stands, and they do this by placing the writer on a mental map of familiar options: the writer agrees with those he or she is responding to, disagrees with them, or presents some combination of both agreeing and disagreeing.

When writers take too long to declare their position relative to views they've summarized or quoted, readers get frustrated, wondering, "Is this guy agreeing or disagreeing? Is he *for* what this other person has said, against it, or what?" For this reason, this chapter's advice applies to reading as well as to writing. Especially with difficult texts, you not only need to find the position the writer is responding to—the "they say"—but you also need to determine whether the writer is agreeing with it, challenging it, or both.

Perhaps you'll worry that fitting your own response into one of these three categories will force you to oversimplify your argument or lessen its complexity, subtlety, or originality. In fact, however, the more complex and subtle your argument is, and the more it departs from the conventional ways people think, the more your readers will need to be able to place it on their mental map in order to process the complex details you present. That is, the complexity, subtlety, and originality of your response are more likely to stand out and be noticed if readers have a baseline sense of where you stand relative to any ideas you've cited. As you move through this chapter, we hope you'll agree that the forms of agreeing, disagreeing, and both agreeing and disagreeing that we discuss, far from being simplistic or one-dimensional, are able to accommodate a high degree of creative, complex thought.

It is always a good tactic to begin your response not by launching directly into a mass of details, but by stating clearly whether you agree, disagree, or both, using a direct, no-nonsense move such as: "I agree," "I disagree," or "I am of two minds. I agree that _____, but I cannot agree that _____." Once you have offered one of these straightforward statements (or one of the many variations discussed below), readers will have a strong grasp of your position and then be able to appreciate whatever complexity you offer as your response unfolds.

Still, you may object that these three basic ways of responding don't cover all the options—that they ignore interpretive or analytical responses, for example. In other words, you might think that when you interpret a literary work you don't necessarily agree or disagree with anything, but simply explain the work's meaning, style, or structure. Many essays about literature and the arts, it might be said, take this form—they interpret a work's meaning, thus rendering matters of agreeing or disagreeing irrelevant.

We would argue, however, that the best interpretations do in fact agree, disagree, or both—that instead of being offered solo, the best interpretations take strong stands relative to other interpretations. In fact, there would be no reason to offer an interpretation of a work of literature or art unless you were responding to the interpretations or possible interpretations of others. Even when you point out features or qualities of an artistic work that others have not noticed, you are implicitly disagreeing with what those interpreters have said by pointing out that they missed or overlooked something that, in your view, is important. In any effective interpretation, then, you need to not only state what you yourself take the work of art to mean, but to do so relative to the interpretations of other readers—be they professional scholars, teachers, classmates, or even hypothetical readers (as in, "Although some readers might think that this poem is about _____, it is in fact about _____").

DISAGREE—AND EXPLAIN WHY

Disagreeing may seem like one of the simpler moves a writer can make, but in fact it poses hidden challenges. You need to do more than simply assert that you disagree with a particular view; you also have to offer persuasive reasons *why* you disagree. After all, disagreeing means more than adding "not" to what someone else has said, more than just saying, "Although they say women's rights are improving, I say women's rights are not improving." Such a response merely contradicts the view it responds to and fails to add anything interesting or new. To make an argument, you need to give reasons why you disagree: because another's argument fails to take relevant factors into account; because it is based on faulty or incomplete evidence; because it rests on questionable assumptions; or because it uses flawed logic, is contradictory, or overlooks what you take to be the real issue. To move the conversation forward (and, indeed, to justify your very act of writing), you need to demonstrate that you yourself have something to contribute.

You can even disagree by making what we call the "duh" move, in which you disagree not with the position itself but with the assumption that it is a new or stunning revelation. Here is an example of such a move, used to open a 2003 essay on the state of American schools.

> According to a recent report by some researchers at Stanford University, high school students with college aspirations "often lack crucial information on applying to college and on succeeding academically once they get there."
> Well, duh. . . . It shouldn't take a Stanford research team to tell us that when it comes to "succeeding academically," many students don't have a clue.
>
> GERALD GRAFF, "Trickle-Down Obfuscation"

Like all of the other moves discussed in this book, the "duh" move can be tailored to meet the needs of almost any writing situation. If you find the expression "duh" too brash to use with your intended audience, you can always dispense with the term itself and write something like "It is true that . . . ; but we already knew that."

TEMPLATES FOR DISAGREEING, WITH REASONS

▶ I think X is mistaken because she overlooks _____.

▶ X's claim that _____ rests upon the questionable assumption that _____.

▶ I disagree with X's view that _____ because, as recent research has shown, _____.

▶ X contradicts herself/can't have it both ways. On the one hand, she argues _____. But on the other hand, she also says _____.

▶ By focusing on _____, X overlooks the deeper problem of _____.

▶ X claims _____, but we don't need him to tell us that. Anyone familiar with _____ has long known that _____.

You can also disagree by making what we call the "twist it" move, in which you agree with the evidence that someone else has presented, but show through a twist of logic that this evidence actually supports your own position. For example:

> X argues for stricter gun control legislation, saying that the crime rate is on the rise and that we need to restrict the circulation of guns. I agree that the crime rate is on the rise, but that's precisely why I oppose stricter gun control legislation. We need to own guns to protect ourselves against criminals.

In this example of the "twist it" move, the writer agrees with X's claim that the crime rate is on the rise, but then argues that this increasing crime rate is in fact a valid reason for *opposing* gun control legislation.

At times you might be reluctant to express disagreement, for any number of reasons—not wanting to be unpleasant, to hurt someone's feelings, or to make yourself vulnerable to being disagreed with in return. One of these reasons may in fact explain why the conference speaker we describe at the start of Chapter 1 avoided mentioning the disagreement he had with other scholars until he was provoked to do so in the discussion that followed his talk.

As much as we understand this reluctance and have felt it ourselves, we nevertheless believe it is better to state our disagreements in frank yet considerate ways than to deny them. After all, suppressing disagreements doesn't make them go away; it only pushes them underground, where they can fester in private unchecked. Nevertheless, there is no reason why disagreements need to take the form of personal put-downs. Furthermore, there is usually no reason to take issue with *every* aspect of someone else's views. You can single out for criticism only those aspects of what someone else has said that are troubling, and then agree with the rest—although that situation, as we will see, leads to the somewhat more complicated terrain of both agreeing and disagreeing at the same time, taken up later in this chapter.

AGREE—BUT WITH A DIFFERENCE

Like disagreeing, agreeing is less simple than it may appear. Just as you need to avoid simply contradicting views you disagree with, you also need to do more than simply echo views you agree with. Even as you're agreeing, it's important to bring something new and fresh to the table, adding something that makes you a valuable participant in the conversation.

There are many moves that enable you to contribute something of your own to a conversation even as you agree with what someone else has said. You may point out some unnoticed evidence or line of reasoning that supports X's claims that X herself hadn't mentioned. You may cite some corroborating personal experience, or a situation not mentioned by X that her views help readers understand. If X's views are particularly challenging or esoteric, what you bring to the table could be an accessible translation—an explanation for readers not already in the know. In other words, your text can usefully contribute to the conversation simply by pointing out unnoticed implications or explaining something that needs to be better understood.

Whatever mode of agreement you choose, the important thing is to open up some difference between your position and the one you're agreeing with rather than simply parroting what it says.

TEMPLATES FOR AGREEING

▶ I agree that .... because my experience .... confirms it.

▶ X is surely right about .... because, as she may not be aware, recent studies have shown that ....

▶ X's theory of .... is extremely useful because it sheds insight on the difficult problem of ....

▶ I agree that ...., a point that needs emphasizing since so many people believe ....

▶ Those unfamiliar with this school of thought may be interested to know that it basically boils down to ....

Some writers avoid the practice of agreeing almost as much as others avoid disagreeing. In a culture like America's that prizes originality, independence, and competitive individualism, writers sometimes don't like to admit that anyone else has made the same point, seemingly beating them to the punch. In our view, however, as long as you can support a view taken by someone else without merely restating what he or she has said, there is no reason to worry about being "unoriginal." Indeed, there is good reason to rejoice when you agree with others since those others can lend credibility to your argument. While you don't want to present yourself as a mere copycat of someone else's views, you also need to avoid sounding like a lone voice in the wilderness.

But do be aware that whenever you agree with one person's view, you are most likely disagreeing with someone else's. It is hard to align yourself with one position without at least implicitly positioning yourself against others. The feminist psychologist Carol Gilligan does just that in an essay in which she agrees with scientists who argue that the human brain is "hard-wired" for cooperation, but in so doing aligns herself against anyone who believes that the brain is wired for selfishness and competition.

> These findings join a growing convergence of evidence across the human sciences leading to a revolutionary shift in consciousness. . . . If cooperation, typically associated with altruism and self-sacrifice, sets off the same signals of delight as pleasures commonly associated with hedonism and self-indulgence; if the opposition between selfish and selfless, self vs. relationship biologically makes no sense, then a new paradigm is necessary to reframe the very terms of the conversation.
>
> CAROL GILLIGAN, "Sisterhood Is Pleasurable: A Quiet Revolution in Psychology"

In agreeing with some scientists that "the opposition between selfish and selfless . . . makes no sense," Gilligan implicitly disagrees with anyone who thinks the opposition *does* make sense. Basically, what Gilligan says could be boiled down to a template.

▸ I agree that _____, a point that needs emphasizing since so many people believe _____.

▸ If group X is right that _____, as I think they are, then we need to reassess the popular assumption that _____.

What such templates allow you to do, then, is to agree with one view while challenging another—a move that leads into the domain of agreeing and disagreeing simultaneously.

AGREE AND DISAGREE SIMULTANEOUSLY

This last option is often our favorite way of responding. One thing we particularly like about agreeing and disagreeing simultaneously is that it helps us get beyond the kind of "is too"/"is not" exchanges that often characterize the disputes of young children and the more polarized shouting matches of talk radio and TV.

TEMPLATES FOR AGREEING
AND DISAGREEING SIMULTANEOUSLY

"Yes and no." "Yes, but . . . " "Although I agree up to a point, I still insist . . . " These are just some of the ways you can make your argument complicated and nuanced while maintaining a clear, reader-friendly framework. The parallel structure—"yes and no"; "on the one hand I agree, on the other I disagree"—enables readers to place your argument on that map of positions we spoke of earlier while still keeping your argument sufficiently complex.

Another aspect we like about this option is that it can be tipped subtly toward agreement or disagreement, depending on where you lay your stress. If you want to stress the disagreement end of the spectrum, you would use a template like the one below.

▸ Although I agree with X up to a point, I cannot accept his overall conclusion that _____.

Conversely, if you want to stress your agreement more than your disagreement, you would use a template like this one.

▸ Although I disagree with much that X says, I fully endorse his final conclusion that _____.

The first template above might be called a "yes, but . . . " move, the second a "no, but . . . " move. Other versions include the following.

▸ Though I concede that _____, I still insist that _____.

▸ X is right that _____, but she seems on more dubious ground when she claims that _____.

▸ While X is probably wrong when she claims that _____, she is right that _____.

▸ Whereas X provides ample evidence that _____, Y and Z's research on _____ and _____ convinces me that _____ instead.

Another classic way to agree and disagree at the same time is to make what we call an "I'm of two minds" or a "mixed feelings" move.

▶ I'm of two minds about X's claim that _____ . On the one hand, I agree that _____ . On the other hand, I'm not sure if

_____ .

▶ My feelings on the issue are mixed. I do support X's position that _____ , but I find Y's argument about _____ and Z's research on _____ to be equally persuasive.

This move can be especially useful if you are responding to new or particularly challenging work and are as yet unsure where you stand. It also lends itself well to the kind of speculative investigation in which you weigh a position's pros and cons rather than come out decisively either for or against. But again, as we suggest earlier, whether you are agreeing, disagreeing, or both agreeing and disagreeing, you need to be as clear as possible, and making a frank statement that you are ambivalent is one way to be clear.

Nevertheless, many writers are as reluctant to express ambivalence as they are to disagree or agree. Some may worry that by expressing ambivalence they will come across as evasive, wishy-washy, or unsure of themselves. Or they may think that their ambivalence will end up confusing readers who require clear-cut statements. In fact, however, expressing ambivalent feelings can serve to demonstrate deep sophistication as a writer. There is nothing wrong with forthrightly declaring that you have mixed feelings, especially after you've considered various options. Indeed, although you never want to be merely evasive, leaving your ambivalence thoughtfully unresolved can demonstrate your integrity as a writer, showing that you are not easily satisfied with viewing complex subjects in simple yes-or-no terms.

Exercises

1. Read the following passage by Jean Anyon, an education professor at Rutgers University, Newark. As you'll see, she summarizes the arguments of several other authors before moving on to tell us what she thinks. Does she agree with those she summarizes, disagree, or some combination of both? How do you know?

Scholars in political economy and the sociology of knowledge have recently argued that public schools in complex industrial societies like our own make available different types of educational experience and curriculum knowledge to students in different social classes. Bowles and Gintis, for example, have argued that students in different social-class backgrounds are rewarded for classroom behaviors that correspond to personality traits allegedly rewarded in the different occupational strata—the working classes for docility and obedience, the managerial classes for initiative and personal assertiveness. Basil Bernstein, Pierre Bourdieu, and Michael W. Apple, focusing on school knowledge, have argued that knowledge and skills leading to social power and regard (medical, legal, managerial) are made available to the advantaged social groups but are withheld from the working classes, to whom a more "practical" curriculum is offered (manual skills, clerical knowledge). While there has been considerable argumentation of these points regarding education in England, France, and North America, there has been little or no attempt to investigate these ideas empirically in elementary or secondary schools and classrooms in this country.

This article offers tentative empirical support (and qualification) of the above arguments by providing illustrative examples of differences in student *work* in classrooms in contrasting social-class communities. . . .

Jean Anyon, "Social Class and the Hidden Curriculum of Work"

2. Read one of the essays at the back of this book, underlining places where the author agrees with others, disagrees, or both. Then write an essay of your own, responding in some way to the essay. You'll want to summarize and/or quote some of the author's ideas and make clear whether you're agreeing, disagreeing, or both agreeing and disagreeing with what he or she says. Remember that there are templates in this book that can help you get started; see Chapters 1–3 for templates that will help you represent other people's ideas, and Chapter 4 for templates that will get you started with your response.

FIVE

"AND YET"

Distinguishing What You Say from What They Say

——⊡——

IF GOOD ACADEMIC writing involves putting yourself into dialogue with others, it is extremely important that readers be able to tell at every point when you are expressing your own view and when you are stating someone else's. This chapter takes up the problem of moving from what *they* say to what *you* say without confusing readers about who is saying what.

DETERMINE WHO IS SAYING WHAT IN THE TEXTS YOU READ

Before examining how to signal who is saying what in your own writing, let's look at how to recognize such signals when they appear in the texts you read—an especially important skill when it comes to the challenging works assigned in school. Frequently, when students have trouble understanding difficult texts, it is not just because the texts contain unfamiliar ideas or words, but because they rely on subtle clues to let readers know when a particular view should be attributed to the writer or to someone else. Especially with texts that present a true dialogue of perspectives, readers need to be alert to the often subtle markers that indicate whose voice the writer is speaking in.

Consider how the social critic and educator Gregory Mantsios uses these "voice markers," as they might be called, to distinguish the different perspectives in his essay on America's class inequalities.

> "We are all middle-class," or so it would seem. Our national consciousness, as shaped in large part by the media and our political leadership, provides us with a picture of ourselves as a nation of prosperity and opportunity with an ever expanding middle-class life-style. As a result, our class differences are muted and our collective character is homogenized.
>
> Yet class divisions are real and arguably the most significant factor in determining both our very being in the world and the nature of the society we live in.
>
> GREGORY MANTSIOS, "Rewards and Opportunities:
> The Politics and Economics of Class in the U.S."

Although Mantsios makes it look easy, he is actually making several sophisticated rhetorical moves here that help him distinguish the common view he opposes from his own position.

In the opening sentence, for instance, the phrase "or so it would seem" shows that Mantsios does not necessarily agree with the view he is describing, since writers normally don't present views they themselves hold as ones that only "seem" to be true. Mantsios also places this opening view in quotation marks to signal that it is not his own. He then further distances himself from the belief being summarized in the opening paragraph by attributing it to "our national consciousness, as shaped in large part by the media and our political leadership," and then attributing to this "consciousness" a negative, undesirable "result": one in which "our class differences" get "muted" and "our collective character" gets "homogenized," stripped of its diversity and distinctness. Hence, even before Mantsios has declared his own position, readers can get a pretty solid sense of where he probably stands.

Furthermore, the second paragraph opens with the word "yet," indicating that Mantsios is now shifting to his own view (as opposed to the view he has thus far been referring to). Even the parallelism he sets up between the first and second paragraphs—between the first paragraph's claim that class differences do not exist and the second paragraph's claim that they do—helps throw into sharp relief the differences between the two voices. Finally, Mantsios's use of a direct, authoritative, declarative tone in the second paragraph also suggests a switch in voice. Although he does not use the words "I say" or "I argue," he clearly identifies the view he holds by presenting it not as one that merely *seems* to be true or that *others tell us* is true, but as a view that *is* true or, as Mantsios puts it, "real."

These voice markers are an aspect of reading comprehension that is frequently overlooked. Readers who are unfamiliar with them often take an author's summaries of what someone else believes to be an expression of what the author himself or herself believes. Thus when we teach Mantsios's essay, some students invariably come away thinking that the statement "we are all middle-class" is Mantsios's own position rather than the perspective he is opposing, failing to see that in writing these words Mantsios acts as a kind of ventriloquist, mimicking what others say rather than directly expressing what he himself is thinking.

To see how important such voice markers are, consider what the Mantsios passage looks like if we remove them.

> We are all middle-class. . . . We are a nation of prosperity and opportunity with an ever expanding middle-class life-style. . . .
>
> Class divisions are real and arguably the most significant factor in determining both our very being in the world and the nature of the society we live in.

In contrast to the careful delineation between voices in Mantsios's original text, this unmarked version leaves it hard to tell where his voice begins and the voices of others end. With the markers removed, readers would probably not be able to tell that "We are all middle-class" represents a view the author opposes, and that "Class divisions are real" represents what the author himself believes. Indeed, without the markers, readers might well miss the fact that the second paragraph's claim that "Class divisions are real" contradicts the first paragraph's claim that "We are all middle-class."

TEMPLATES FOR SIGNALING WHO IS SAYING WHAT IN YOUR OWN WRITING

To avoid confusion in your own writing, make sure that at every point your readers can clearly tell who is saying what. To do this, you can use as voice-identifying devices many of the templates presented in previous chapters.

▶ X argues _____ .

▶ According to both X and Y, _____ .

▶ Politicians, X argues, should _____ .

▶ Most athletes will tell you that _____ .

▶ My own view, however, is that _____ .

▶ I agree, as X may not realize, that _____ .

When stating your own position, as in the last two templates above, you can generally limit the voice markers to your opening and closing claims, since readers will automatically assume that any declarative statements you make between these statements, unless marked otherwise, are your own.

Notice that the last template above uses the first-person "I," as do many of the templates in this book, thus contradicting the common advice about avoiding the first person in academic and professional writing. Although you may have been told that the "I" word encourages self-indulgent opinions rather than well-grounded arguments, we believe that texts using "I" can be just as well supported—or, conversely, just as self-indulgent—as those that don't. For us, well-supported arguments are grounded in persuasive reasons and evidence, not in their use of any particular pronouns.

Furthermore, if you consistently avoid the first person in your writing, you may have trouble making the key move addressed in this chapter: differentiating your views from those of others, or even offering your own views in the first place. But don't just take our word for it. See for yourself how freely the first person is used by the writers quoted in this book, and also by the writers in your other courses.

Nevertheless, certain occasions may warrant avoiding the first person and writing, for example, that "She is correct" or

"It is a fact that she is correct," instead of "I think that she is correct." And since it can be monotonous to read an unvarying series of "I" statements—"I believe . . . I think . . . I argue"—it is a good idea to mix first-person assertions with ones like the following.

▸ X is right that _____.

▸ The evidence shows that _____.

▸ X's assertion that _____ does not fit the facts.

▸ Anyone familiar with _____ should agree that _____.

One might even follow Mantsios's lead, as in the following template.

▸ But _____ are real, and are arguably the most significant factor in _____.

ANOTHER TRICK FOR IDENTIFYING WHO IS SPEAKING

To alert readers about whose perspective you are describing at any given moment, you don't always have to use overt voice markers like "X argues" followed by a summary of the argument. Instead, you can alert readers about whose voice you're speaking in by *embedding* a reference to X's argument in your own sentences. Hence, instead of writing:

> Liberals believe that cultural differences need to be respected. I have a problem with this view, however.

you might write:

> I have a problem with *what liberals call cultural differences*.

> There is a major problem with the liberal doctrine about *so-called cultural differences*.

You can also embed references to something you yourself have previously said. So instead of writing two cumbersome sentences like:

> Earlier in this chapter we coined the term "voice markers." We would argue that such markers are extremely important for reading comprehension.

you might write:

> We would argue that "voice markers," as we identified them earlier, are extremely important for reading comprehension.

Embedded references like these allow you to economize your train of thought and refer to other perspectives without any major interruption.

TEMPLATES FOR EMBEDDING VOICE MARKERS

▶ X overlooks what I consider an important point about _____ .

▶ My own view is that what X insists is a _____ is in fact a

_____ .

▶ I wholeheartedly endorse what X calls _____ .

▸ These conclusions, which X discusses in _____, add weight
   to the argument that _____.

When writers fail to use voice-marking devices like these, their
summaries of others' views tend to become confused with their
own ideas—and vice versa. When readers cannot tell if you are
summarizing your own views or endorsing a certain phrase or label,
they have to stop and think: "Wait. I thought the author disagreed
with this claim. Has she actually been asserting this view all along?"
or "Hmmm, I thought she would have objected to this kind of
phrase. Is she actually endorsing it?" Getting in the habit of using
voice markers will keep you from confusing your readers and help
alert you to similar markers in the challenging texts you read.

Exercises

1. To see how one writer signals when she is asserting her own
   views and when she is summarizing those of someone else,
   read the following passage by the social historian Julie
   Charlip. As you do so, identify those spots where Charlip
   refers to the views of others and the signal phrases she uses
   to distinguish her views from theirs.

   Marx and Engels wrote: "Society as a whole is more and more splitting up into two great hostile camps, into two great classes directly
   facing each other—the bourgeoisie and the proletariat" (10). If
   only that were true, things might be more simple. But in late twen-
   tieth-century America, it seems that society is splitting more and
   more into a plethora of class factions—the working class, the working poor, lower-middle class, upper-middle class, lower uppers, and
   upper uppers. I find myself not knowing what class I'm from.

In my days as a newspaper reporter, I once asked a sociology professor what he thought about the reported shrinking of the middle class. Oh, it's not the middle class that's disappearing, he said, but the working class. His definition: if you earn thirty thousand dollars a year working in an assembly plant, come home from work, open a beer and watch the game, you are working class; if you earn twenty thousand dollars a year as a school teacher, come home from work to a glass of white wine and PBS, you are middle class.

How do we define class? Is it an issue of values, lifestyle, taste? Is it the kind of work you do, your relationship to the means of production? Is it a matter of how much money you earn? Are we allowed to choose? In this land of supposed classlessness, where we don't have the tradition of English society to keep us in our places, how do we know where we really belong? The average American will tell you he or she is "middle class." I'm sure that's what my father would tell you. But I always felt that we were in some no man's land, suspended between classes, sharing similarities with some and recognizing sharp, exclusionary differences from others. What class do I come from? What class am I in now? As an historian, I seek the answers to these questions in the specificity of my past.

JULIE CHARLIP, "A Real Class Act: Searching
for Identity in the Classless Society"

2. Study a piece of your own writing to see how many perspectives you account for, and how well you distinguish your own voice from those you are summarizing. Consider the following questions:

   a. How many perspectives do you engage?
   b. What other perspectives might you include?

   c. How do you distinguish your views from the other views you summarize?
   d. Do you use clear voice-signaling phrases?
   e. What options are available to you for clarifying who is saying what?
   f. Which of these options are best suited for this particular text?

If you find that you do *not* include multiple views, or clearly distinguish between your views and others', revise your text to do so.

SIX

"Skeptics May Object"

Planting a Naysayer in Your Text

———

THE WRITER JANE TOMPKINS describes a pattern that repeats itself whenever she writes a book or an article. For the first couple of weeks when she sits down to write, things go relatively well. But then in the middle of the night, several weeks into the writing process, she'll wake up in a cold sweat, suddenly realizing that she has overlooked some major criticism that readers will surely make against her ideas. Her first thought, invariably, is that she will have to give up on the project, or that she will have to throw out what she's written thus far and start over. Then she realizes that "this moment of doubt and panic is where my text really begins." She then revises what she's written in a way that incorporates the criticisms she's anticipated, and her text becomes stronger and more interesting as a result.

This little story contains an important lesson for all writers, experienced and inexperienced alike. It suggests that even though most of us are upset at the idea of someone criticizing our work, such criticisms can actually work to our advantage. Although it's naturally tempting to ignore objections to our ideas, doing so may in fact be a big mistake, since everyone's writing actually improves when we not only listen to these objections but give them an explicit hearing in our writing. Indeed, no single device more quickly improves a piece of writing than the practice of planting a naysayer in the text—saying, for example, that "although some readers may object" to something in your argument, you "would reply that _____."

ANTICIPATE OBJECTIONS

But wait, you say. Isn't the advice to incorporate critical views a recipe for destroying your credibility and undermining your argument? Here you are, trying to say something that will hold up, and we want you to tell readers all the negative things someone might say against you?

Exactly. We *are* urging you to tell readers what others might say against you, but our point is that doing so will actually *enhance* your credibility, not undermine it. For as we argue throughout this book, writing well does not mean piling up uncontroversial truths in a vacuum; it means engaging others in a dialogue or debate—not only by opening your text with a summary of what others have to say, as we suggest in Chapter 1, but also by imagining what others might say against your argument as it unfolds. Once you see writing as an act of entering a conversation, you should also see how opposing arguments can work for you rather than against you.

Paradoxically, the more you give voice to your critics' objections, the more you can disarm those critics, especially if you go on to answer them in convincing ways. When you entertain a counter-argument, you make a kind of preemptive strike, identifying problems with your argument before others can point them out for you. Furthermore, by entertaining counterarguments, you show respect for your readers, treating them not as gullible dupes but as independent, critical thinkers who are aware that yours is not the only view in town. In addition, by imagining what others might say against your claims, you come across as a generous, broad-minded person who is secure enough to open himself or herself to debate—like the writer in Figure 5.

Conversely, if you don't entertain counter-arguments, you may very likely come across as closed-minded, as if you think your claims are beyond dispute. You might also leave important questions hanging and concerns about your arguments unaddressed. Finally, if you fail to plant a naysayer in your text, you may find that you have very little to say. Many of our own students have said that entertaining counter-arguments makes it easier to generate enough text to meet their assignment's page-length requirements.

Planting a naysayer in your own text is a relatively simple move, as you can see by looking at the following passage from a book by the feminist writer Kim Chernin. Having spent some thirty pages complaining about the pressure on American women to lose weight and be thin, Chernin inserts a whole chapter entitled "The Skeptic," opening it as follows.

> At this point I would like to raise certain objections that have been inspired by the skeptic in me. She feels that I have been ignoring some of the most common assumptions we all make about our bodies and these she wishes to see addressed. For example: "You know perfectly well," she says to me, "that you feel better when you lose weight. You buy new clothes. You look at yourself more eagerly in the mirror. When someone invites you to a party you don't stop and ask yourself whether you want to go. You feel sexier. Admit it. You like yourself better."
>
> KIM CHERNIN, *The Obsession:*
> *Reflections on the Tyranny of Slenderness*

FIGURE 5

In the remainder of the chapter, Chernin answers this skeptic. Though Chernin's inner skeptic challenges her book's central claim (that the pressure to diet seriously harms women's lives), she responds not by repressing its voice but by embracing it and writing it into her text. Note too that instead of dispatching this naysaying voice quickly, as many of us would be tempted to do, Chernin stays with it and gives it a full paragraph's worth of space. By borrowing some of Chernin's language, we can come up with templates for entertaining virtually any objection.

TEMPLATES FOR ENTERTAINING OBJECTIONS

▸ At this point I would like to raise some objections that have been inspired by the skeptic in me. She feels that I have been ignoring _____. "_____," she says to me, "_____."

▸ Yet some readers may challenge my view that _____. After all, many believe that _____. Indeed, my own argument that _____ seems to ignore _____ and _____.

▸ Of course, many will probably disagree with this assertion that _____.

Note that the objections in the above templates are attributed not to any specific person or group, but to "skeptics," "readers," or "many." This kind of nameless, faceless naysayer is perfectly appropriate in many cases. But the ideas that motivate arguments and objections often can—and, where possible, should—be ascribed to a specific ideology or school of thought (for example, liberals, Christian fundamentalists, neopragmatists) rather than to anonymous anybodies. In other words, naysayers can be labeled, and you can add precision and impact to your writing by identifying what they are.

TEMPLATES FOR NAMING YOUR NAYSAYERS

► Here many *feminists* would probably object that _____.

► But *social Darwinists* would certainly take issue with the argument that _____.

► *Biologists*, of course, may want to dispute my claim that _____.

► Nevertheless, both *followers and critics of Malcolm X* will probably suggest otherwise and argue that _____.

To be sure, some people dislike such labels and may even resent having them applied to themselves. Some feel that such labels put individuals in boxes, stereotyping them and glossing over what makes each individual unique. And it's true that labels can be used inappropriately, in ways that ignore individuality and promote stereotypes. But since the life of ideas, including many of our most private thoughts, is conducted through groups and types rather than by solitary individuals, intellectual exchange requires labels to give definition and serve as a convenient shorthand. If you categorically reject all labels, you give up an important resource and even mislead readers by presenting yourself and others as having no connection to anyone else. You also miss an opportunity to generalize the importance and relevance of your work to some larger conversation. When you attribute a position you are summarizing to liberalism, say, or racial separatism, your argument is no longer just about your own solitary views, but about the intersection of broad ideas and habits of mind that many readers already have a stake in.

The way to minimize the problem of stereotyping, then, is not to categorically reject labels but to refine and qualify their use, as the following templates demonstrate.

▸ Although not all *Christians* think alike, some of them will probably dispute my claim that _____ .

▸ *Non-native English speakers* are so diverse in their views that it's hard to generalize about them, but some are likely to object on the grounds that _____ .

Another way to avoid needless stereotyping is to qualify labels carefully, substituting "pro bono lawyers" for "lawyers" in general, for example, or "quantitative sociologists" for all "sociologists," and so on.

TEMPLATES FOR INTRODUCING OBJECTIONS INFORMALLY

Objections can also be introduced in ways that are a bit more informal. For instance, you can frame objections in the form of questions.

▸ But is my proposal realistic? What are the chances of its actually being adopted?

▸ Yet is it always true that _____ ? Is it always the case, as I have been suggesting, that _____ ?

▸ However, does the evidence I've cited prove conclusively that _____ ?

You can also let your naysayer speak directly.

▶ "Impossible," you say. "Your evidence must be skewed."

Moves like this allow you to cut directly to the skeptical voice itself, as the singer-songwriter Joe Jackson does in the following excerpt from a 2003 *New York Times* article complaining about the restrictions on public smoking in New York City bars and restaurants.

> I like a couple of cigarettes or a cigar with a drink, and like many other people, I only smoke in bars or nightclubs. Now I can't go to any of my old haunts. Bartenders who were friends have turned into cops, forcing me outside to shiver in the cold and curse under my breath. . . . It's no fun. Smokers are being demonized and victimized all out of proportion.
>
> "Get over it," say the anti-smokers. "You're the minority." I thought a great city was a place where all kinds of minorities could thrive. . . . "Smoking kills," they say. As an occasional smoker with otherwise healthy habits, I'll take my chances. Health consciousness is important, but so are pleasure and freedom of choice.
>
> JOE JACKSON, "Want to Smoke? Go to Hamburg"

Jackson could have begun his second paragraph, in which he shifts from his own voice to that of his imagined naysayer, as follows: "Of course anti-smokers will object that since we smokers are in the minority, we should get over it and sacrifice for the larger social good." Or "Anti-smokers might ask, however, whether the smoking minority shouldn't submit to the non-smoking majority." We think, however, that Jackson gets the job done very well with the more colloquial form he chooses.

Borrowing a standard move of playwrights and novelists, Jackson cuts directly to the objectors' view and then to his own retort, then back to the objectors' view and then to his own retort again, thereby creating a kind of dialogue or miniature play within his own text. This move works well for Jackson, but only because (using one of the strategies suggested in Chapter 5) he uses quotation marks to make clear at every point whose voice he is in.

REPRESENT OBJECTIONS FAIRLY

Once you've decided to introduce a differing or opposing view into your writing, your work has only just begun, since you still need to represent and explain that view with fairness and generosity. Although it is tempting to give opposing views short shrift, to hurry past them, or even to mock them, doing so is usually counterproductive. When writers make the best case they can for their critics (playing what Peter Elbow calls the "believing game"), they actually bolster their credibility with readers, rather than undermine it.

We recommend, then, that whenever you entertain objections in your writing you stay with them for several sentences or even paragraphs and take them as seriously as possible. We also recommend that you read your summary of opposing views with an outsider's eye: put yourself in the shoes of someone who disagrees with you and ask if such a reader would recognize himself in your summary. Would that reader think you have taken his views seriously, as beliefs that reasonable people might hold? Or would he detect a mocking tone, or an oversimplification of his views?

There will always be certain objections, to be sure, that you believe do not deserve to be represented, just as there will be objections that seem so unworthy of respect that they inspire ridicule. Remember, however, that if you do choose to mock a view that you oppose, you are likely to alienate those readers who don't already agree with you—likely the very readers you want to reach. Also be aware that in mocking another's view you may contribute to a hostile argument culture in which someone could ridicule you in return.

ANSWER OBJECTIONS

Finally, besides summarizing objections fairly in your writing, you need to answer those objections persuasively. After all, when you write objections into a text, you always take the risk that readers will find those objections more convincing than the argument you yourself are advancing. In the editorial quoted above, for example, Joe Jackson takes the risk that non-smokers will identify more with the anti-smoking view he summarizes than with the pro-smoking position he endorses. Another case in point is presented in *The Autobiography of Benjamin Franklin* (1868), where at one point Franklin recounts how he was converted to Deism (a religion that exalts reason over spirituality) by reading *anti*-Deist books. When he encountered the views of Deists being negatively summarized by authors who opposed them, Franklin ended up finding the Deist position more persuasive. To avoid having this kind if unintentional reverse effect on readers, you need to do your best to make sure that any counter-argument you address is not more convincing than your own claims. It is good to address objections in your writing, but only if you are able to overcome them.

One surefire way to *fail* to overcome an objection is to dismiss it out of hand—saying, for example, "That's just wrong." The difference between such a response (which offers no supporting reasons whatsoever) and the types of nuanced responses we're promoting in this book is the difference between bullying your readers and genuinely persuading them.

Often the best way to overcome an objection is not to try to refute it completely, but to agree with certain parts while challenging only those you dispute. In other words, in answering counter-arguments, it is often best to say "yes, but" or "yes and no," as we suggest in Chapter 4, treating the counter-view as an opportunity to revise and refine your own position. Rather than building your argument into an impenetrable fortress, it is often best to make concessions while still standing your ground, as Kim Chernin does in the following response to the counter-argument quoted above. While in the voice of the "skeptic," Chernin writes: "Admit it. You like yourself better when you've lost weight." In response, Chernin replies as follows.

> Can I deny these things? No woman who has managed to lose weight would wish to argue with this. Most people feel better about themselves when they become slender. And yet, upon reflection, it seems to me that there is something precarious about this well-being. After all, 98 percent of people who lose weight gain it back. Indeed, 90 percent of those who have dieted "successfully" gain back more than they ever lost. Then, of course, we can no longer bear to look at ourselves in the mirror.

In this way, Chernin shows how you can use a counter-view to improve and refine your overall argument by making a concession. Even as she concedes that losing weight feels good in the short run, she argues that in the long run the weight always returns, making the dieter far more miserable.

TEMPLATES FOR MAKING CONCESSIONS WHILE STILL STANDING YOUR GROUND

▸ Although I grant that _____, I still maintain that _____.

▸ Proponents of X are right to object that _____. But they exaggerate when they claim that _____.

▸ While it is true that _____, it does not necessarily follow that _____.

▸ On the one hand, I agree with the liberal view that _____. But on the other hand, I still insist that _____.

Templates like these show that answering naysayers' objections does not have to be an all-or-nothing affair in which you either definitively refute your critics or they definitively refute you. Often the most productive engagements among differing views end with a combined vision that incorporates elements of each one.

But what if you've tried out all the possible answers you can think of to an objection you've anticipated and you *still* have a nagging feeling that the objection is more convincing than your argument itself? In that case, the best remedy is to go back and make some fundamental revisions to your argument, changing its very substance. Although finding out late in the game that you aren't fully convinced by your own argument can be painful, it can actually make your final text more intellectually honest, challenging, and serious. After all, the goal of writing is not to keep proving that whatever you initially said is right, but to stretch the limits of your thinking. So if planting a strong naysayer in your text forces you to change your mind, that's not a bad thing. Indeed, some would argue that that is what school and learning are all about.

Exercises

1. Read the following passage by the cultural critic Eric Schlosser. As you'll see, he's not planted any naysayers in this text. Do it for him. Insert a brief paragraph stating an objection to his argument and then responding to the objection as he might.

   The United States must declare an end to the war on drugs. This war has filled the nation's prisons with poor drug addicts and small-time drug dealers. It has created a multibillion-dollar black market, enriched organized crime groups and promoted the corruption of government officials throughout the world. And it has not stemmed the widespread use of illegal drugs. By any rational measure, this war has been a total failure.

   We must develop public policies on substance abuse that are guided not by moral righteousness or political expediency but by common sense. The United States should immediately decriminalize the cultivation and possession of small amounts of marijuana for personal use. Marijuana should no longer be classified as a Schedule I narcotic, and those who seek to use marijuana as medicine should no longer face criminal sanctions. We must shift our entire approach to drug abuse from the criminal justice system to the public health system. Congress should appoint an independent commission to study the harm-reduction policies that have been adopted in Switzerland, Spain, Portugal, and the Netherlands. The commission should recommend policies for the United States based on one important criterion: what works.

In a nation where pharmaceutical companies advertise powerful antidepressants on billboards and where alcohol companies run amusing beer ads during the Super Bowl, the idea of a "drug-free society" is absurd. Like the rest of American society, our drug policy would greatly benefit from less punishment and more compassion.

ERIC SCHLOSSER, "A People's Democratic Platform"

2. Look over something you've written that makes an argument. Check to see if you've anticipated and responded to any objections. If not, revise your text to do so. If so, have you anticipated all the likely objections? What group if any have you attributed the objections to? Have you represented it fairly? Have you answered the objections well enough, or do you think you now need to qualify your own argument? Did you use any of the language found in this chapter's templates? Does the introduction of a naysayer strengthen your argument—why, or why not?

SEVEN

"So What? Who Cares?"

Saying Why It Matters

———

BASEBALL IS THE national pastime. Bernini was the best sculptor of the baroque period. Evolution is central to the teaching of biology. So what? Who cares? Why does any of this matter?

How many times have you had reason to ask—or answer—these questions? Regardless of how interesting a topic may be to you as a writer, readers always need to know what is at stake in a text and why they should care. All too often, however, these questions are left unanswered—mainly because writers and speakers assume that audiences will know or will figure out the answers on their own. As a result, students come away from lectures feeling like outsiders to what they've just heard, and their own instructors come away from academic conferences feeling alienated by many of the presentations. The problem is not necessarily that these talks lack a clear, well-focused thesis, or that the thesis is inadequately supported with evidence. Instead, the problem is that the speakers don't address the crucial question of why their arguments matter.

That this crucial question is so often left unaddressed is unfortunate since the speakers generally *could* offer interesting, engaging answers. When pressed, for instance, most academics will tell you that their lectures and articles matter because they address some belief that needs to be corrected or updated—and because their arguments have important, real-world consequences. Yet many academics fail to explicitly identify these reasons and consequences in what they say and write. Rather than assume that audiences will know why their claims matter, all writers need to answer the "so what?" and "who cares?" questions up front. Not everyone can claim to have a cure for cancer or a solution to end poverty. But writers who cannot show that others *should* care and *do* care about their claims will ultimately lose their audiences' interest.

This chapter focuses on various moves that you can make to answer the "who cares?" and "so what?" questions in your own writing. In one sense, the two questions get at the same thing: the relevance or importance of what you are saying. Yet they get at this significance in different ways. Whereas "who cares?" literally asks you to identify a person or group who cares about your claims, "so what?" asks about the real-world applications and consequences of those claims—what difference it would make if they were accepted. We'll look first at ways of making clear who cares.

"Who Cares?"

To see how one writer answers the "who cares?" question, consider the following passage from the science writer Denise Grady. Writing in the *New York Times*, she explains some of the latest research into fat cells.

> Scientists used to think body fat and the cells it was made of were pretty much inert, just an oily storage compartment. But within the past decade research has shown that fat cells act like chemi-

cal factories and that body fat is potent stuff: a highly active tissue that secretes hormones and other substances with profound and sometimes harmful effects. . . .

In recent years, biologists have begun calling fat an "endocrine organ," comparing it to glands like the thyroid and pituitary, which also release hormones straight into the bloodstream.

DENISE GRADY, "The Secret Life of a Potent Cell"

Notice how Grady's writing reflects the central advice we give in this book, offering a clear claim and also framing that claim as a response to what someone else has said. In so doing, Grady immediately identifies at least one group with a stake in the new research that sees fat as "active," "potent stuff": namely, the scientific community, which formerly believed that body fat is inert. By referring to these scientists, Grady implicitly acknowledges that her text is part of a larger conversation and shows who besides herself has an interest in what she says.

Consider, however, how the passage would read had Grady left out what "scientists used to think" and simply explained the new findings in isolation.

Within the past few decades research has shown that fat cells act like chemical factories and that body fat is potent stuff: a highly active tissue that secretes hormones and other substances. In recent years, biologists have begun calling fat an "endocrine organ," comparing it to glands like the thyroid and pituitary, which also release hormones straight into the bloodstream.

Though this statement is clear and easy to follow, it lacks any indication that anyone needs to hear it. Okay, one nods while reading this passage, fat is an active, potent thing. Sounds plausible enough; no reason to think it's not true. But does anyone really care? Who, if anyone, is interested?

TEMPLATES FOR INDICATING WHO CARES

To address "who cares?" questions in your own writing, we suggest using templates like the following, the first of which mimics Grady's style in the *New York Times*.

▸ _____ used to think _____. But recently [or within the past few decades] _____ suggests that _____.

▸ This interpretation challenges the work of those critics who have long assumed that _____.

▸ These findings challenge the work of earlier researchers, who tended to assume that _____.

▸ Recent studies like these shed new light on _____, which previous studies had not addressed.

Grady might have been more explicit by writing the "who cares?" question directly into her text, as in the following template.

▸ But who really cares? Who besides me and a handful of recent researchers has a stake in these claims? At the very least, the researchers who assumed that fat _____ should care.

To gain greater authority as a writer, it helps to name specific people or groups who have a stake in your claims and to go into some detail about their views.

▸ Researchers have long assumed that _____. For instance, one eminent scholar of cell biology, _____, assumed in _____, her seminal work on cell structures and functions, that fat cells _____. As _____ herself put it, "_____" (200–).

Another leading scientist, _____, argued that fat cells "_____" (200-). Ultimately, when it came to the nature of fat, the basic assumption was that _____.

But a new body of research shows that fat cells are far more complex and that _____.

In other cases, you might refer to certain people or groups who *should* care about your claims.

▸ If sports enthusiasts stopped to think about it, many of them might simply assume that the most successful athletes _____. However, new research shows _____.

▸ These findings challenge the common assumption among corporate leaders that _____.

▸ At first glance, teenagers might say _____. But on closer inspection _____.

Such templates help you to generate interest in your subject by identifying populations of readers who are likely to have a stake in it.

"So What?"

Although answering the "who cares?" question is crucial, in many cases it is not enough, especially if you are writing for general readers who don't necessarily have a strong investment in your subject (as Grady is in the *New York Times*). In the case of Grady's argument about fat cells, such readers may still wonder why it matters that some researchers think fat cells are active and others think they're inert. Or, to move to a different field of study, *so what* if some scholars disagree about Huck Finn's relationship with the runaway slave Jim? Why should anyone besides a few specialists in the field care about such disputes? What, if anything, hinges on them?

The best way to answer such questions about the larger consequences of your claims is to appeal to something that your audience already figures to care about. Whereas the "who cares?" question asks you to identify an interested person or group, the "so what?" question asks you to link your argument to some larger matter that readers already deem important. Thus in analyzing *Huckleberry Finn*, a writer could argue that seemingly narrow disputes about the hero's relationship with Jim actually shed light on what Twain's canonical, widely read novel says about racism in America.

Let's see how Grady invokes such broad, general concerns in her article on fat cells. Her first move is to link researchers' interest in fat cells to a general concern with obesity and health.

> Researchers trying to decipher the biology of fat cells hope to find new ways to help people get rid of excess fat or, at least, prevent obesity from destroying their health. In an increasingly obese world, their efforts have taken on added importance.

Further showing why readers should care, Grady's next move is to demonstrate the even broader relevance and urgency of her subject matter.

> Internationally, more than a billion people are overweight. Obesity and two illnesses linked to it, heart disease and high blood pressure, are on the World Health Organization's list of the top 10 global health risks. In the United States, 65 percent of adults weigh too much, compared with about 56 percent a decade ago, and government researchers blame obesity for at least 300,000 deaths a year.

What Grady implicitly says here is: "Look, dear reader, you may think that these questions about the nature of fat cells I've been pursuing have little to do with everyday life. In fact, however, these questions are extremely important—particularly "in an increasingly obese world" in which we need to minimize obesity's ill effects."

Notice that Grady's phrase "in an increasingly _____ world" can be adapted as a strategic move to address the "so what?" question in other fields as well. For example, a sociologist analyzing back-to-nature movements of the past thirty years might make the following statement.

> In a world increasingly dominated by cellphones and sophisticated computer technology, these attempts to return to nature and simplify one's life are extremely significant forms of protest.

This type of move can be readily applied to other disciplines because no matter how much these disciplines may differ, the need to justify the importance of one's concerns is common to them all.

TEMPLATES FOR ESTABLISHING WHY YOUR CLAIMS MATTER

▶ X matters/is important because _____.

▶ Although X may seem trivial, it is in fact crucial in terms of today's concern over _____.

▶ Ultimately, what is at stake here is _____.

▸ These findings have important consequences for the broader domain of _____.

▸ My discussion of X is in fact addressing the larger matter of _____.

▸ These conclusions/This discovery will have significant applications in _____ as well as in _____.

Finally, you can also treat the "so what?" question as a related aspect of the "who cares?" question.

▸ Although X may seem of concern to only a small group of _____, it should in fact concern anyone who cares about _____.

All these templates help you to hook your readers. By suggesting the real-world applications of your claims, the templates not only demonstrate that others care about your claims but also tell your readers why *they* should care. Again, it bears repeating that simply stating and proving your thesis isn't enough. You also need to frame it in a way that helps readers care about it.

WHAT ABOUT READERS WHO ALREADY KNOW WHY IT MATTERS?

At this point, you might wonder if you need to answer the "who cares?" and "so what?" questions in *everything* you write. Is it really necessary to address these questions if you're proposing something so obviously consequential as, say, a cure for a childhood disease or a program to eliminate illiteracy? Isn't it obvious that everyone cares about such problems? Does it really need to be spelled out? And what about when you're writing for audiences who you already know are interested in your claims and who understand perfectly well why they're important? In other words, do you always need to address the "so what?" and "who cares?" questions?

As a rule, yes—although it's true that you can't keep answering them forever and at a certain point must say enough is enough. Although a determined skeptic can infinitely ask why something matters—"Who cares about dieting?" And then, "Who cares about health?"—you have to stop answering at some point in your text. Nevertheless, we urge you to go as far as possible in answering such questions. If you ignore them or give them short shrift, you run the risk that readers will dismiss your text as irrelevant and unimportant. And though some expert readers might already know why your claims matter, even they may need to be reminded that they know it. Thus the safest move is to be as explicit as possible in answering the "so what?" question, even for those already in the know.

If you take it for granted that readers will somehow intuit the answers to "so what?" and "who cares?" on their own, you may make your work seem less interesting and exciting than it actually is. Therefore we suggest that whether you are offering a cure for cancer or trying to change the way we read Walt Whitman's poetry, be sure to present what you're saying *as* a cure for cancer or a challenge to how Whitman's poetry is read. When you are careful to explain who cares and why, it's a little like bringing a cheerleading squad into your text. When you step back from the text—a move that we discuss in Chapter 10—and explain why it matters, you are urging your audience to keep reading, pay attention, and care.

Exercises

1. Read several articles and essays to see whether they address the "so what?" and "who cares?" questions. Probably you'll find that some do, some don't. The question to consider then is whether it makes a difference to you as a reader. Are those texts that say why it matters more interesting? More persuasive?

2. Look over something you've written yourself. Do you indicate "so what?" and "who cares?"? If not, revise your text to do so. You might use the following template to get started.

▶ My point here—that _____—should interest those who _____. Beyond this limited audience, however, my point should speak to anyone who cares about the larger issue of _____.

3

TYING IT ALL
TOGETHER

EIGHT

"As a Result"

Connecting the Parts

———◘———

WE ONCE HAD a student named Bill, whose characteristic sentence pattern went something like this.

> Spot is a good dog. He has fleas.

"Connect your sentences," we urged in the margins of Bill's papers. "What does Spot being good have to do with his fleas? These two statements seem unrelated. Can you connect them in some logical way?" When such comments yielded no results, we tried inking in suggested connections for him.

> Spot is a good dog, *but* he has fleas.
> Spot is a good dog, *even though* he has fleas.

But our message failed to get across, and Bill's disconnected sentence pattern persisted to the end of the semester.

And yet, Bill did focus well on his subjects. When he mentioned Spot the dog in one sentence, we could count on Spot the dog being the topic of the following sentence as well. This was not the case with some of Bill's classmates, who sometimes changed topic from sentence to sentence or even from clause to clause within a single sentence. But because Bill neglected to mark his connections, his writing was as frustrating to read as theirs. In all these cases, we had to struggle to figure out on our own how the sentences and paragraphs connected or failed to connect with each other.

What makes such writers so hard to read, in other words, is that they never gesture back to what they have just said or forward to what they plan to say. "Never look back" might be their motto, almost as if they see writing as a process of thinking of something to say about a topic and writing it down, then thinking of something else to say about the topic and writing that down too, and on and on until they've filled the assigned number of pages and can hand the paper in. Each sentence basically starts a new thought, rather than growing out of or extending the thought of the previous sentence.

When Bill talked about his writing habits, he acknowledged that he never went back and read what he had written. Indeed, he told us that, other than using his computer software to check for spelling errors and make sure that his tenses were all aligned, he never actually reread what he wrote before turning it in. Writing for Bill was just that: something he did while sitting at a computer. Reading, including rereading, was a separate activity generally reserved for an easy chair, book in hand. It had never occurred to Bill that to write a good sentence he had to think about how it connected to those that came before and after it; that he had to think hard about the relationship among the sentences he wrote. Each sentence for Bill existed in a sort of tunnel isolated from every other sentence on the page. He never bothered to fit all the parts of his essay together because he apparently thought of writing as a matter of piling up information or insights rather than building an argument.

What we suggest in this chapter, then, is that you converse not only with others in your writing, but with yourself: that you establish clear relations between one statement and the next by connecting those statements together.

This chapter addresses the issue of how to connect all the parts of your writing. The best compositions establish a sense of momentum and direction by making explicit connections among their different parts, so that what is said in one sentence (or paragraph) not only sets up what is to come but is clearly informed by what has already been said. When you write a sentence, you create an expectation in the reader's mind that the next sentence will in some way echo and be an extension of the first, even if—*especially if*—the second one takes your argument in a new direction.

It may help to think of each sentence you write as having arms that reach backward and forward, as Figure 6 suggests. When your sentences reach outward like this, they establish connections that help your writing flow smoothly in a way readers appreciate. Conversely, when writing lacks such connections and moves in fits and starts, readers repeatedly have to go back over the sentences and guess at the connections on their own. To prevent such disconnection and make your writing flow, we advise following a "do it yourself" principle, which means that it is your

FIGURE 6

job as a writer to do the hard work of making the connections rather than, as Bill did, leaving this work to your readers.

This chapter offers several moves you can make to put this principle into action: (1) using transition terms (like "therefore" and "yet"); (2) adding pointing words (like "this" or "such"); (3) using certain key terms and phrases throughout your entire text; and (4) repeating yourself, but with a difference—a move that involves repeating elements in your previous sentence, but with enough variation to move the text forward and without being redundant. All these moves require that you always look back and, in crafting any one sentence, think hard about those that precede it.

Notice how we ourselves have used such connecting devices thus far in this chapter. The second paragraph of this chapter, for example, opens with the transitional "And yet," signaling a change in direction, while the third includes the phrase "in other words," telling you to expect a restatement of a point we've just made. If you look through this book, you should be able to find many sentences that contain some word or phrase that explicitly hooks them back to something said earlier, to something about to be said, or both. And many sentences in *this* chapter repeat key terms related to the idea of connection: "connect," "disconnect," "link," "relate," "forward," and "backward."

Use Transitions

For readers to follow your train of thought, you need not only to connect your sentences and paragraphs to each other, but also to mark the kind of connection you are making. One of the easiest ways to make this move is to use *transitions* (from the Latin root *trans ire*, "to cross over"), which help you to cross from one point to another in your text. Transitions are usually placed at or near the start of sentences so they can signal to readers where your text is going: in the same direction it has been moving, or in a new direction. More specifically, transitions tell readers whether your text is echoing a previous sentence or paragraph ("in other words"), adding something to it ("in addition"), offering an example of it ("for example"), generalizing from it ("as a result"), or modifying it ("and yet").

The following is a list of commonly used transition terms, categorized according to their different functions.

ADDITION also, and, besides, furthermore, in addition, indeed, in fact, moreover, so too

EXAMPLE after all, as an illustration, for example, for instance, specifically, to take a case in point

ELABORATION actually, by extension, that is, in other words, to put it another way

COMPARISON along the same lines, in the same way, likewise, similarly

CONTRAST although, but, by contrast, conversely, despite the fact that, even though, however, in contrast, nevertheless, nonetheless, on the contrary, on the other hand, regardless, whereas, while, yet

CAUSE AND EFFECT accordingly, as a result, because, consequently, hence, in effect, since, so, then, therefore, thus

CONCESSION admittedly, although it is true, granted, naturally, of course, to be sure

CONCLUSION as a result, consequently, hence, in conclusion, in short, in sum, therefore, thus, to sum up, to summarize, ultimately, to put it bluntly

Ideally, transitions should operate so unobtrusively in a piece of writing that they recede into the background and readers do not even notice that they are there. It's a bit like what happens when drivers use their turn signals before turning right or left: just as other drivers recognize such signals almost unconsciously, readers should process transition terms with a minimum of thought. But even though such terms should function unobtrusively in your writing, they can be among the most powerful tools in your vocabulary. Think how your heart sinks when someone, immediately after praising you, begins a sentence with "but" or "however." No matter what follows, you know it won't be good.

Notice that some transitions can help you not only to move from one sentence to another, but to combine two or more sentences into one. Combining sentences in this way helps prevent the choppy, staccato effect that arises when too many short sentences are strung together, one after the other. For instance, to combine Bill's two choppy sentences ("Spot is a good dog. He has fleas.") into one, better-flowing sentence, we suggested that he rewrite them as: "Spot is a good dog, *even though* he has fleas."

Transitions like these not only guide readers through the twists and turns of your argument, but also help ensure that you *have* an argument to begin with. In fact, we think of words like "but," "yet," "nevertheless," "besides," and others as argument words, since it's hard to use them without making some kind of argument. The word "therefore," for instance, commits you to making sure that the claims leading up to it lead logically to the conclusion that it introduces. "For example" also assumes an argument, since it requires that the material you are introducing stand as an instance or a proof of some preceding generalization. As a result, the more you use transitions, the more you'll be able not only to connect the parts of your text but also to construct a strong argument in the first place.

While you don't need to memorize these transitions, we do suggest that you draw on them so frequently that using them eventually becomes second nature. To be sure, it is possible to overuse these terms, so take time to read over your drafts carefully and eliminate any transitions that are unnecessary. But following the maxim that one needs to learn the basic moves of argument before one can deliberately depart from them, we advise you not to forgo explicit transition terms until you've first mastered their use. In all our years of teaching, we've read countless essays that suffered from having few or no transitions, but we have yet to receive one in which the transitions were overdone. Seasoned writers often do without explicit transitions, but only because they rely heavily on the other types of connecting devices that we turn to in the rest of this chapter.

Before doing so, however, let us warn you about inserting transitions without really thinking through their meanings—using "therefore," say, when your text's logic actually requires "nevertheless" or "however." So beware. Choosing transition terms should involve a bit of mental sweat, since the whole point of using them is to make your writing *more* reader-friendly, not less. The only thing more frustrating than reading Bill-style passages like "Spot is a good dog. He has fleas" is reading misconnected sentences like "Spot is a good dog. For example, he has fleas."

USE POINTING WORDS

Another move you can make to connect the parts of your argument is to use pointing words—which, as their name implies, point or refer backward to some concept in the previous sentence. The most common of these pointing words include "this,"

"these," "that," "those," "their," and "such" (as in "these pointing words" near the start of this sentence) and simple pronouns
like "his," "he," "her," "she," "it," and "their." Such terms help
you create the flow we spoke of earlier that enables readers to
move effortlessly through your text. In a sense, these terms are
like an invisible hand reaching out of your sentence, grabbing
what's needed in the previous sentences and pulling it along.

Like transitions, however, pointing words need to be used
carefully. It's dangerously easy to insert pointing words into your
text that don't refer to a clearly defined object, thinking that
because the object you have in mind is clear to you it will also
be clear to your readers. For example, consider the use of "this"
in the following passage.

> Alexis de Tocqueville was highly critical of democratic societies,
> which he saw as tending toward mob rule. At the same time,
> he accorded democratic societies grudging respect. *This* is seen in
> Tocqueville's statement that . . .

When "this" is used in such a way it becomes an ambiguous or
free-floating pointer, since readers can't tell if it refers to Tocque-
ville's critical attitude toward democratic societies, his grudging respect for them, or some combination of both. "This what?"
readers mutter as they go back over such passages and try to
figure out your meaning.

You can fix such problems caused by a free-floating pointer
by making sure there is one and only one possible object in the
vicinity that the pointer could be referring to. It also often helps
to name the object the pointer is referring to at the same time
that you point to it, replacing a bald "this," for instance, with
a more precise phrase like "this ambivalence toward democratic
societies" or "this grudging respect."

REPEAT KEY TERMS AND PHRASES

A third move you can make to connect the parts of your argument is to develop a constellation of key terms and phrases, including their synonyms and antonyms, that you repeat throughout your text. Used well, key terms even provide readers with some sense of your topic. Playing with key terms also is a good way to develop a title and appropriate section headings for your text.

For an example of a move that effectively incorporates key terms, notice how often Martin Luther King Jr. uses the key words "criticism(s)" and "statement" in the opening paragraph to his famous "Letter from Birmingham Jail."

> Dear Fellow Clergymen:
>
> While confined here in the Birmingham city jail, I came across your recent *statement* calling my present activities "unwise and untimely." Seldom do I pause to answer *criticism* of my work and ideas. If I sought to answer all the *criticisms* that cross my desk, my secretaries would have little time for anything other than *such correspondence* in the course of the day, and I would have no time for constructive work. But since I feel that you are men of genuine good will and that your *criticisms* are sincerely set forth, I want to try to answer your *statement* in what I hope will be patient and reasonable terms.
>
> MARTIN LUTHER KING JR., "Letter from Birmingham Jail"

Even though King uses the term "criticism(s)" three times and "statement" twice, the effect is not overly repetitive. In fact, these key terms help bind the paragraph together. And though King does not explicitly use those terms in the remainder of his letter, he keeps the concepts in play by elab-

orately summarizing each of the specific criticisms laid out
against him in the statement he has received and then
answering them.

For another example of the effective use of key terms, consider the following passage from *Where the Girls Are: Growing
Up Female with the Mass Media,* in which the feminist historian
Susan Douglas develops a constellation of sharply contrasting
key terms around the concept of cultural schizophrenics:
women like herself who, Douglas claims, have mixed feelings
about the images of ideal femininity with which they are constantly bombarded by the media.

> In a variety of ways, the mass media helped make us the critical
> schizophrenics we are today, women who rebel against yet submit
> to prevailing images about what a desirable, worthwhile woman
> should be. . . . [T]he mass media has engendered in many women a
> kind of cultural identity crisis. We are ambivalent toward feminin-
> ity on the one hand and feminism on the other. Pulled in opposite
> directions—told we were equal, yet told we were subordinate; told
> we could change history but told we were trapped by history—we
> got the bends at an early age, and we've never gotten rid of them.
>
> When I open *Vogue,* for example, I am simultaneously infuri-
> ated and seduced. . . . I adore the materialism; I despise the mate-
> rialism. . . . I want to look beautiful; I think wanting to look
> beautiful is about the most dumb-ass goal you could have. The mag-
> azine stokes my desire; the magazine triggers my bile. And this
> doesn't only happen when I'm reading *Vogue*; it happens all the
> time. . . . On the one hand, on the other hand—that's not just
> me—that's what it means to be a woman in America.
>
> To explain this schizophrenia . . .
>
> SUSAN DOUGLAS, *Where the Girls Are:*
> *Growing Up Female with the Mass Media*

In this passage, Douglas establishes "schizophrenia" as a key concept and then echoes it through synonyms like "identity crisis," "ambivalent," "the bends"—and even demonstrates it through a series of contrasting words and phrases:

> rebel against / submit
> told we were equal / told we were subordinate
> told we could change history / told we were trapped by history
> infuriated / seduced
> I adore / I despise
> I want / I think wanting . . . is about the most dumb-ass goal
> stokes my desire / triggers my bile
> on the one hand / on the other hand

These contrasting phrases help explain Douglas's claim that women are being pulled in two directions at once. In so doing, they bind the passage together into a unified whole that, despite its complexity and sophistication, stays focused over its entire length.

REPEAT YOURSELF—BUT WITH A DIFFERENCE

The last move we offer for connecting the parts of your text involves repeating yourself, but with a difference—which basically means saying the same thing you've just said, but in a slightly different way that avoids sounding monotonous. To effectively connect the parts of your argument and keep it moving forward, be careful not to leap from one idea to a different idea or introduce new ideas cold. Instead, try to build bridges between your ideas by echoing what you've just said while simultaneously moving your text into new territory.

Several of the connecting devices discussed in this chapter are ways of repeating yourself in this special way. Key terms, pointing terms, and even many transitions can be used in a way that not only brings something forward from the previous sentence, but in some way alters it. When Douglas, for instance, uses the key term "ambivalent" to echo her earlier reference to schizophrenia, she is repeating herself with a difference—repeating the same concept, but with a different word that adds new associations. When she uses a pointing term in "this schizophrenia," she is also repeating herself with a difference by explicitly naming the conflicting psychological and emotional responses she had earlier outlined but had not labeled.

In addition, when you use transition phrases like "in other words" and "to put it another way," you repeat yourself with a difference, since these phrases help you restate earlier claims in a different register. When you open a sentence with "in other words," you are basically telling your readers that in case they didn't fully understand what you meant in the last sentence, you are now coming at it again from a slightly different angle; or that since you're presenting a very important idea, you're not going to skip over it quickly but will explore it further to make sure your readers grasp all its aspects.

We would even go so far as to suggest that after your first sentence, almost every sentence you write should include some form of repetition, but with a difference. Whether you are writing a "furthermore" comment that adds to what you have just said or a "for example" statement that illustrates it, each sentence should echo at least one element of the previous sentence in some discernible way. Even when your text changes direction and requires transitions like "in contrast," "however," or "but," you still need to mark that shift by link-

ing the sentence to the one just before it, as in the following
example.

> The girl loved basketball. Nevertheless, she feared her height would
> put her at a disadvantage.

These sentences work because even though the second sentence changes course and qualifies the first, it still echoes key
concepts from the first. Not only does "she" echo "the girl,"
since both refer to the same person, but "feared" echoes "loved"
by establishing the contrast mandated by the term "nevertheless." "Nevertheless," then, is not an excuse for changing subjects radically. It too requires a little repetition to help readers
shift gears with you and follow your train of thought.

Repetition, in short, is the central means by which you can
move from point A to point B in a text. To introduce one last
analogy, think of the way experienced rock climbers move up
a steep slope. Instead of jumping or lurching from one handhold to the next, good climbers get a secure handhold on the
position they have established before reaching for the next
ledge. The same thing applies to writing. To move smoothly
from point to point in your argument, you need to firmly ground
what you say in what you've already said. In this way, your writing remains focused while simultaneously moving forward.

Exercises

1. Read the following passage from the conclusion to a PhD
   dissertation focusing on the rags-to-riches stories of the
   American Industrial Revolution. Underline all the con-

necting devices—transitions, pointing terms, key terms, and repetition. For each one, explain how it helps you to read and understand the argument.

The most remarkable thing to me about the American Dream of rags-to-riches success is the extent to which most people think they understand it. The idea that America is a fair, open society that rewards merit (regardless of one's gender, race, or class background), and that individuals control their own economic fate is so pervasive that, like the air we breathe, it can easily be taken for granted. Even critics who expose the idea of individual responsibility as a lie or myth—as an instance of propaganda that unfairly blames the poor for their poverty and legitimates wealth, and that thwarts collective political action—usually assume that they are dealing with a set, already known entity. My goal in this dissertation, however, has been to defamiliarize this deeply familiar story and show that, in many (though not all) its formulations, the American rags-to-riches story contains unexpected complexities and divisions that, largely because of their unexpectedness, have been widely overlooked.

> CATHY BIRKENSTEIN, *Rereading the American Rags-to-Riches Story: Conflict and Contradiction in the Works of Horatio Alger, Booker T. Washington, and Willa Cather*

2. Read over something you've written with an eye for the devices you've used to connect the parts. Underline all the transitions, pointing terms, key terms, and repetition. Do you see any patterns? Do you rely on certain devices more than others? Are there any passages that are hard to follow—and if so, can you make them easier to read by adding appropriate transitions or trying any of the other devices discussed in this chapter? If there are any devices you don't use at all, try revising your text to try them out.

NINE

"Ain't So / Is Not"

Academic Writing Doesn't Mean Setting Aside Your Own Voice

———⟐———

HAVE YOU EVER GOTTEN the impression that writing well in college means setting aside the kind of language you use in everyday conversation? That to impress your instructors you need to use big words, long sentences, and complex sentence structures? If so, then we're here to tell you that it ain't necessarily so. On the contrary, academic writing can—and in our view *should*—be relaxed, easy to follow, and even a little bit fun. Although we don't want to suggest that you avoid using sophisticated, academic terms in your writing, we encourage you to draw upon the kinds of expressions and turns of phrase that you use every day when conversing with family and friends. In this chapter, we want to show you how you can write effective academic arguments while at the same time holding on to some of your own voice.

This point is important, since you may well become turned off from writing if you think your everyday language practices have to be checked at the classroom door. You may end up feeling like a student we know who, when asked how she felt about the writing she does in college, answered, "I do it because I have to, but it's just not me!"

This is not to suggest that *any* language you use among friends has a place in writing. Nor is it to suggest that you may fall back on colloquial usage as an excuse for not learning more rigorous forms of expression. It is, however, to suggest that relaxed, colloquial language can often enliven academic writing and even enhance its rigor and precision. Such informal language also helps you to connect with readers in a personal as well as an intellectual way. In our view, then, it is a mistake to assume that academic writing and everyday language are completely separate things, and that they can never be used together.

MIX ACADEMIC AND COLLOQUIAL STYLES

Many successful writers blend academic, professional language with popular expressions and sayings. Consider, for instance, the following passage from a scholarly article about the way teachers respond to errors in student writing.

> Marking and judging formal and mechanical errors in student papers is one area in which composition studies seems to have a multiple-personality disorder. On the one hand, our mellow, student-centered, process-based selves tend to condemn marking formal errors at all. Doing it represents the Bad Old Days. Ms. Fidditch and Mr. Flutesnoot with sharpened red pencils, spilling innocent blood across the page. Useless detail work. Inhumane, perfectionist standards, making our students feel stupid, wrong, trivial, misunderstood. Joseph Williams has pointed out how arbitrary and context-bound our judgments of formal error are. And certainly our noting of errors on student papers gives no one any

great joy; as Peter Elbow says, English is most often associated *either* with grammar or with high literature—"two things designed to make folks feel most out of it."

ROBERT CONNORS AND ANDREA LUNSFORD,
"Frequency of Formal Errors in Current College Writing,
or Ma and Pa Kettle Do Research"

This passage blends writing styles in several ways. First, it places informal, relaxed expressions like "mellow," "the Bad Old Days," and "folks" side-by-side with more formal, academic-sounding phrases like "multiple-personality disorder," "student-centered," "process-based," and "arbitrary and context-bound." Even the title of the piece, "Frequency of Formal Errors in Current College Writing, or Ma and Pa Kettle Do Research," blends formal, academic usage on the left side of the comma with a popular-culture reference to the fictional movie characters Ma and Pa Kettle on the right. Second, to give vivid, concrete form to their discussion of grading disciplinarians, Connors and Lunsford conjure up such imaginary figures as the stuffy, old-fashioned task-masters Ms. Fidditch and Mr. Flutesnoot. Through such imaginative uses of language, Connors and Lunsford inject greater force into what might otherwise have been dry, scholarly prose.

Formal/informal mixings like this can be found in countless other texts. Notice how the food industry critic Eric Schlosser describes some changes in the city of Colorado Springs in his best-selling book on fast foods in the United States.

> The loopiness once associated with Los Angeles has come full blown to Colorado Springs—the strange, creative energy that crops up where the future's consciously being made, where people walk the fine line separating a visionary from a total nutcase.

ERIC SCHLOSSER, *Fast Food Nation*

Schlosser could have played it safe and referred not to the "loopiness" but to the "eccentricity" associated with Los Angeles, or to "the fine line separating a visionary from a lunatic" instead of " . . . a total nutcase." His decision, however, to go with the more adventuresome, colorful terms gives a liveliness to his writing that would have been lacking with the more conventional terms.

Another example of writing that blends the informal with the formal comes from an essay on the American novelist Willa Cather by the literary critic Judith Fetterley. Discussing "how very successful Cather has been in controlling how we think about her," Fetterley, building on the work of another scholar, writes as follows.

> As Merrill Skaggs has put it, "She is neurotically controlling and self-conscious about her work, but she knows at all points what she is doing. Above all else, she is self-conscious."
>   Without question, Cather was a control freak.
>
> JUDITH FETTERLEY, "Willa Cather and the
> Question of Sympathy: The Unofficial Story"

This passage demonstrates not only that specialized, psychological phrases like "neurotically controlling" and "self-conscious" are compatible with everyday, popular expressions like "control freak," but also that translating the one type of language into the other, the specialized into the everyday, can help drive home a point. By translating Skaggs's academic description of Cather as "neurotically controlling and self-conscious" into the succinct claim that "Without question, Cather was a control freak," Fetterley suggests that one need not choose between specialized, academic ways of talking and the everyday language of casual conversation. Indeed, her passage offers a simple recipe for blending the specialized and the everyday: first make your point in the language of a professional field, and then make it again in everyday language—a great trick, we think, for underscoring a claim.

Although one reason to blend languages like this is to give your writing more punch, another reason is to make a political statement—about the way, for example, society unfairly over-values some varieties of language and devalues others. For instance, in the titles of two of her books, *Talkin and Testifyin: The Language of Black America* and *Black Talk: Words and Phrases from the Hood to the Amen Corner*, the language scholar Geneva Smitherman mixes African American vernacular phrases with more scholarly language in order to suggest, as she explic-itly argues in these books, that black English vernacular is as legitimate a variety of language as "standard" English. Here are three typical passages.

> In Black America, the oral tradition has served as a fundamen-tal vehicle for gittin ovuh. That tradition preserves the Afro-American heritage and reflects the collective spirit of the race.
>
> Blacks are quick to ridicule "educated fools," people who done gone to school and read all dem books and still don't know nothin!
>
> . . . it is a socially approved verbal strategy for black rappers to talk about how bad they is.
>
> —GENEVA SMITHERMAN, *Talkin and Testifyin: The Language of Black America*

In these examples, Smitherman blends the standard written English of phrases like "oral tradition" and "fundamental vehi-cle" with black oral vernacular like "gittin ovuh," "dem books," and "how bad they is." Indeed, she even blends standard English spelling with that of black English variants like "dem" and "ovuh," thus mimicking what some black English vernacular actually sounds like. Although some scholars might object to these unconventional practices, this is precisely Smitherman's point: that our habitual language practices need to be opened up, and that the number of participants in the academic conversation needs to be expanded.

Along similar lines, the writer and activist Gloria Anzaldúa mixes standard English with Tex-Mex, a hybrid blend of English, Castilian Spanish, a North Mexican dialect, and the Indian language Nahuatl, to make a political point about the suppression of the Spanish language in the United States.

> From this racial, ideological, cultural, and biological cross-pollinization, an "alien" consciousness is presently in the making—a new *mestiza* consciousness, *una conciencia de mujer.*
>
> —GLORIA ANZALDÚA,
> *Borderlands / La Frontera: The New Mestiza*

Like Smitherman, Anzaldúa gets her point across not only through what she says, but through the way she says it, literally showing that the new hybrid, or *mestiza*, consciousness that she describes is, as she puts it, "presently in the making."

WHEN TO MIX STYLES?
CONSIDER YOUR AUDIENCE AND PURPOSE

Because there are so many options in writing, you should never feel limited in your choice of words, as if such choices are set in stone. You can always play with your language and improve it. You can always dress it up, dress it down, or some combination of both. In dressing down your language, for example, you can make the claim that somebody "failed to notice" something by saying instead that it "flew under her radar." You can state that somebody was "unaware" of something by saying that he was "out to lunch." You could even recast the title of this book, "*They Say/I Say*," as a teenager might say it: "I'm Like/She Goes."

But how do you know when it is better to play things straight and stick to standard English, and when to be more adventuresome and mix things up? When, in other words, should you write "failed to notice" and when is it okay (or more effective) to write "flew under her radar"? Is it *always* appropriate to mix styles? And when you do so, how do you know when enough is enough?

In all situations, think carefully about your audience and purpose. When you write a letter applying for a job, for instance, or submit a grant proposal, where your words will be weighed by an official screening body, using language that's too colloquial or slangy may well jeopardize your chances of success. On such occasions, it is usually best to err on the safe side, conforming as closely as possible to the conventions of standard written English. In other situations for other audiences, however, there is room to be more creative—in this book, for example. Ultimately, your judgments about the appropriate language for the situation should always take into account your likely audience and your purpose in writing.

Although it may have been in the past, academic writing today is no longer the linguistic equivalent of a black-tie affair. To succeed as a writer in college, then, you need not limit your language to the strictly formal; you need not abandon your own voice. Although academic writing does rely on complex sentence patterns and on specialized, disciplinary vocabularies, it is surprising how often such writing draws on the languages of the street, popular culture, our ethnic communities, and home. It is by blending these languages that "standard" English changes over time and the range of possibilities open to all writers continues to grow.

Exercises

1. Take a paragraph from this book and dress it down, rewriting it in informal colloquial language. Then rewrite the same paragraph again by dressing it up, making it much more formal. Then rewrite the paragraph one more time in a way that blends the two styles. Share your paragraphs with a classmate, and discuss which one you prefer and why.

2. Find something you've written for a course, and study it to see whether you've used any of your own everyday expressions, any words or structures that are not "academic." If by chance you don't find any, see if there's a place or two where shifting into more casual or unexpected language would help you make a point, get your reader's attention, or just add a little liveliness to your text. Be sure to keep your audience and purpose in mind, and use language that will be appropriate to both.

TEN

"In Other Words"

The Art of Metacommentary

—▱—

WHENEVER WE TELL PEOPLE that we are writing a chapter on the art of metacommentary, many of them give us a puzzled look and tell us that they have no idea what "metacommentary" is. "We know what commentary is," they'll sometimes say, "but what does it mean when it's *meta*?" Our answer is that they may not know the term, but they probably practice the art of metacommentary on a daily basis whenever they make a point of explaining something they've said or written: "What I meant to say was _____," "My point was not _____, but _____," or "You're probably not going to like what I'm about to say, but _____." In such cases, people are not offering new points, but telling an audience how to interpret what they have already said or are about to say. In terms of writing, then, metacommentary is a way of commenting on your claims and telling readers how—and how *not*—to think about them.

It may help to think of metacommentary as being like the chorus in a Greek play that stands apart from the drama unfolding on the stage and explains its meaning to the audience—or like a voice-over narrator who comments on and explains the action in a television show or movie. Like a Greek chorus or narrator, metacommentary is a sort of second text that stands alongside your main text and explains what it means. In the main text you say something; in the metatext you help readers interpret and process what you've said.

What we are suggesting, then, is that you think of your text as two texts joined at the hip: a main text in which you make your argument, and another in which you "work" your ideas, distinguishing your views from others they may be confused with, anticipating and answering objections, connecting one point to another, explaining why your claim might be controversial, and so forth—in short, guiding readers in processing and interpreting your main points. Figure 7 demonstrates what we mean.

THE MAIN TEXT SAYS SOMETHING, THE METATEXT
TELLS READERS HOW—AND HOW NOT—TO READ IT.

FIGURE 7

USE METACOMMENTARY TO CLARIFY AND ELABORATE

But why do you need metacommentary to tell readers what you mean and guide them through your text? Can't you just clearly *say* what you mean up front? In fact, no matter how clear and precise your writing is, readers can still fail to understand you in any number of ways. Even the best writers can provoke reactions in readers that they didn't intend, and even good readers can get lost in a complicated argument or fail to see how one point connects with another. Readers may also fail to see what follows from your argument, or they may follow your reasoning and examples yet fail to see the larger conclusion you draw from them. They may fail to see your argument's overall significance, or mistake what you are saying for a related claim that you actually want to distance yourself from. As a result, no matter how clear a writer you are, readers still need you to help them process what you really mean. Because the written word is prone to so much mischief and can be interpreted in so many different ways, we need metacommentary to keep misinterpretations and other communication misfires at bay.

Another reason to master the art of metacommentary is that it will help you develop your ideas and generate more text. If you have ever had trouble producing the required number of pages for a writing project, metacommentary can help you add both length and depth to your writing. We've seen many students try to produce a five-page paper but then sputter to a halt at two or three pages, complaining they've said everything they can think of about their topic. "I've stated my thesis and presented my reasons and evidence," students have told us. "What else is there to do?" It's almost as if such writers have generated a thesis and don't know what to do with it. When these students learn to use metacommentary, however, they get more out of their ideas and write longer, more substantial texts. In sum, metacommentary can help you "work" your ideas, drawing out important implications, explaining the ideas from a different angle, clarifying how one idea supports another, and so forth.

So, even when you may think you've said everything possible in an argument, try inserting the following types of metacommentary.

▶ In other words, _____.

▶ What _____ really means is _____.

▶ This is not to say _____.

When you begin making these metacommentary moves in your writing, we predict you'll be happily surprised at how they'll help to bring out implications of your ideas that you didn't even realize were there.

Let's look at how the cultural critic Neil Postman uses metacommentary in the following passage describing the shift he sees in American culture as it moves away from print and reading to television and movies.

> *It is my intention in this book to show* that a great . . . shift has taken place in America, with the result that the content of much of our public discourse has become dangerous nonsense. *With this in view, my task in the chapters ahead is* straightforward. *I must, first, demonstrate* how, under the governance of the printing press, discourse in America was different from what it is now—generally coherent, serious and rational; *and then* how, under the governance of television, it has become shriveled and absurd. *But to avoid the possibility that my analysis will be interpreted as* standard-brand academic whimpering, a kind of elitist complaint against "junk" on televi-

sion, *I must first explain that* . . . I appreciate junk as much as the
next fellow, *and I know full well that* the printing press has generated enough of it to fill the Grand Canyon to overflowing. Television is not old enough to have matched printing's output of junk.

NEIL POSTMAN, *Amusing Ourselves to Death:*
Public Discourse in the Age of Show Business

To see what we mean by metacommentary, look at the phrases
above that we have italicized. With these moves, Postman
essentially stands apart from his main ideas to help readers see
their implications.

Previewing what he will argue: *It is my intention in this book*
to show . . .

Spelling out how he will make his argument: *With this in*
view, my task in these chapters . . . *is.* . . . *I must, first, demon-*
strate . . . *and then* . . .

Distinguishing his argument from other arguments it may
easily be confused with: *But to avoid the possibility that my*
analysis will be interpreted as . . . *I must first explain that* . . .

TITLES AS METACOMMENTARY

Even the title of Postman's book, *Amusing Ourselves to Death:*
Public Discourse in the Age of Show Business, functions as a form
of metacommentary since, like any title, it stands apart from
the text itself and tells readers the book's main point: that,
while amusing, show business has created what Postman suggests is a destructive form of public discourse.

Titles, in fact, are one of the most important forms of metacommentary, functioning rather like carnival barkers telling

passersby what they can expect if they go inside. Subtitles, too often function as metacommentary on a main title, further explaining or elaborating on it. The subtitle of this book, for example, not only explains that this book is about "the moves that matter in persuasive writing," but indicates that "they say/ I say" is one of these moves. Thinking of a title as metacommentary can actually help you to develop sharper titles, leading you to write something that gives readers some sense of your argument rather than merely announcing your topic, or that it's an "English Essay"—or having no title at all. Essays that bear no title send the message that the writer has simply not bothered to reflect on what he or she is saying.

USE OTHER MOVES AS METACOMMENTARY

Many of the other moves covered in this book function as metacommentary: entertaining objections, adding transitions, framing quotations, answering "so what?" and "who cares?" When you entertain objections, you stand outside your text and imagine what a critic might say; when you add transitions, you essentially explain the relationship between various claims. And when you answer the "so what?" and "who cares?" questions, you look beyond your central argument and explain who cares about it and why.

TEMPLATES FOR INTRODUCING METACOMMENTARY

TO WARD OFF POTENTIAL MISUNDERSTANDINGS

This move differentiates your view from ones it might be mistaken for.

▸ But don't misunderstand me. My point is not _____, but _____.

▸ I concede, of course, that _____. Nevertheless, _____.

TO ALERT READERS TO AN ELABORATION OF A PREVIOUS IDEA

This move says to readers: "In case you didn't get it the first time, I'll try saying the same thing in a different way."

▸ In other words, _____.

▸ To put it another way, _____.

TO PROVIDE READERS WITH A ROADMAP TO YOUR TEXT

This move orients readers, giving them advance notice about where you are going and making it easier for them to process and follow your text.

▸ Chapter 2 explores _____, while Chapter 3 examines _____.

▸ Having just argued that _____, let us now turn our attention to _____.

TO MOVE FROM A GENERAL CLAIM TO A SPECIFIC EXAMPLE

This move signals that you are about to offer a concrete example that illustrates what you're saying.

▸ For example, _____.

▸ _____, for instance, demonstrates _____.

▸ Consider _____, for example.

▸ To take a case in point, _____.

TO INDICATE THAT A CLAIM IS ESPECIALLY IMPORTANT, OR LESS IMPORTANT

This move shows that what you are about to say is either more or less important than what you just said.

▸ Even more important, _____ .

▸ But above all, _____ .

▸ Incidentally, _____ .

▸ By the way, _____ .

TO HELP YOU ANTICIPATE AND RESPOND TO AN OBJECTION

This move helps you imagine and respond to other viewpoints.

▸ Although some readers may object that _____ , I would answer that _____ .

TO GUIDE READERS TO YOUR MOST GENERAL POINT

This move shows that you are wrapping things up and tying up various subpoints previously made.

▸ In sum, then, _____ .

▸ My conclusion, then, is that _____ .

▸ In short, _____ .

TO ANSWER THE SO WHAT? AND WHO CARES? QUESTIONS

This move helps you identify who cares, or should care, about your argument and why.

▸ This point should be of interest to anyone who _____ .

▸ In making this point, I am challenging the commonly held belief that _____ .

As we note at the start of this chapter, the forms of metacommentary that we recommend, like all the other moves we discuss in this book, are deeply connected to moves you make in everyday conversation. But don't take our word for it. Observe for yourself how writers and speakers use metacommentary—not only in the ways we've mentioned, but in ways that you detect on your own. What you'll notice, we think, is that people don't just make claims, but *work* those claims in various ways, elaborating on them, generalizing from them, and distinguishing them from related claims they might be confused with. The more you become aware of these moves in your reading and everyday life, the more options you'll have to draw on as a writer.

Exercises

1. Complete each of the following metacommentary templates in any way that makes sense.

▸ In making a case for the medical use of marijuana, I am not saying that _____ .

▸ But my argument will do more than prove that one particular industrial chemical has certain toxic properties. In this article, I will also

_____ .

▸ My point about the national obsessions with sports reinforces the belief held by many _____ that _____ .

▶ I believe, therefore, that the war is completely justified. But let me back up and explain how I arrived at this conclusion. _____. In this way, I came to believe that this war is necessary.

2. Read over an essay or article with an eye for metacommentary. Does the writer make any of the moves discussed in this chapter—and if so, how do they affect the success of the argument? Then read over an essay that you've already written to see whether it includes any metacommentary. Start with your title. Does it give readers a good sense of what your text is about? Do you provide any kind of roadmap to where your text will go? Check each of the points you make—do you use metacommentary to elaborate on them? Is your text long enough, or would metacommentary help you to fill it out? Using the templates in this chapter, add at least two instances of metacommentary.

ENTERING CLASS DISCUSSIONS
A BRIEF APPENDIX

—◻︎—

The conversational principles discussed in this book apply to speaking as well as to writing, and in particular to speaking in classroom discussions. But speaking in class has some special requirements, as the following guidelines suggest:

FRAME YOUR COMMENTS AS A RESPONSE TO SOMETHING THAT HAS ALREADY BEEN SAID

Since the best group discussions are genuine conversations rather than a series of disconnected monologues, the single most important thing you need to do when joining a class discussion is to link what you are about to say to something that has already been said:

▶ I really liked the point Aaron made earlier when he said that
   _____. I agree because _____.

▶ I take your point, Nadia, that _____. Still . . .

▶ Though Sheila and Ryan seem to be at odds about _____, they
   may actually not be all that far apart.

In framing your comments this way, it is usually best to name both the person and the idea you're responding to. If you name the person alone ("I agree with Aziz because _____"), it may not be clear to listeners what part of what Aziz said you are referring to.

TO CHANGE THE SUBJECT, INDICATE EXPLICITLY THAT YOU ARE DOING SO

It is fine to try to change the conversation's direction. There's just one catch: you need to make clear to listeners that this is what you are doing. For example:

▶ So far we have been talking about _____. But isn't the real issue here _____?

▶ I'd like to change the subject to one that hasn't yet been addressed.

If you try to change the subject without indicating that you are doing so, your comment will come across as irrelevant rather than as a thoughtful contribution that moves the conversation forward.

BE EVEN MORE EXPLICIT THAN YOU WOULD BE IN WRITING

Because listeners in an oral discussion can't go back and reread what you just said, they are more easily overloaded than are readers of a print text. For this reason, in a class discussion you will do well to take some extra steps to help listeners follow your train of thought. (1) When you make a comment, limit yourself to one point and one point only. Although you can elaborate on this point, fleshing it out with examples and evidence, it is important that any elaboration be clearly focused on your one point. If you feel you must make two points, either unite them under one larger umbrella point, or make one point first and save the other for later. Trying to bundle two or more claims into one comment too often results in neither point getting the attention it deserves. (2) Use metacommentary to highlight your key point:

► In other words, what I'm trying to get at here is _____.

► My point is this: _____.

► My point, though, is not _____, but _____.

► This distinction is important for several reasons: _____.

READINGS

Don't Blame the Eater

DAVID ZINCZENKO

—◩—

IF EVER THERE were a newspaper headline custom-made for Jay Leno's monologue, this was it. Kids taking on McDonald's this week, suing the company for making them fat. Isn't that like middle-aged men suing Porsche for making them get speeding tickets? Whatever happened to personal responsibility?

I tend to sympathize with these portly fast-food patrons, though. Maybe that's because I used to be one of them.

I grew up as a typical mid-1980's latchkey kid. My parents were split up, my dad off trying to rebuild his life, my mom working long hours to make the monthly bills. Lunch and dinner, for me, was a daily choice between McDonald's, Taco Bell, Kentucky Fried Chicken or Pizza Hut. Then as now, these were the only available options for an American kid to get an affordable meal. By age 15, I had packed 212 pounds of torpid teenage tallow on my once lanky 5-foot-10 frame.

Then I got lucky. I went to college, joined the Navy Reserves and got involved with a health magazine. I learned how to manage my diet. But most of the teenagers who live, as I once did,

DAVID ZINCZENKO is the editor-in-chief of *Men's Health*, a monthly magazine that focuses on fitness. This piece was first published on the op-ed page of the *New York Times* on November 23, 2002.

on a fast-food diet won't turn their lives around: They've crossed under the golden arches to a likely fate of lifetime obesity. And the problem isn't just theirs—it's all of ours.

Before 1994, diabetes in children was generally caused by a genetic disorder—only about 5 percent of childhood cases were obesity-related, or Type 2, diabetes. Today, according to the National Institutes of Health, Type 2 diabetes accounts for at least 30 percent of all new childhood cases of diabetes in this country.

Not surprisingly, money spent to treat diabetes has skyrocketed, too. The Centers for Disease Control and Prevention estimate that diabetes accounted for $2.6 billion in health care costs in 1969. Today's number is an unbelievable $100 billion a year.

Shouldn't we know better than to eat two meals a day in fast-food restaurants? That's one argument. But where, exactly, are consumers—particularly teenagers—supposed to find alternatives? Drive down any thoroughfare in America, and I guarantee you'll see one of our country's more than 13,000 McDonald's restaurants. Now, drive back up the block and try to find someplace to buy a grapefruit.

Complicating the lack of alternatives is the lack of information about what, exactly, we're consuming. There are no calorie information charts on fast-food packaging, the way there are on grocery items. Advertisements don't carry warning labels the way tobacco ads do. Prepared foods aren't covered under Food and Drug Administration labeling laws. Some fast-food purveyors will provide calorie information on request, but even that can be hard to understand.

For example, one company's Web site lists its chicken salad as containing 150 calories; the almonds and noodles that come with it (an additional 190 calories) are listed separately. Add a serving of the 280-calorie dressing, and you've got a healthy lunch alternative that comes in at 620 calories. But that's not all. Read the small print on the back of the dressing packet and you'll realize it actually contains 2.5 servings. If you pour what you've been served, you're suddenly up around 1,040 calories, which is half of the government's recommended daily calorie intake. And that doesn't take into account that 450-calorie super-size Coke.

Make fun if you will of these kids launching lawsuits against the fast-food industry, but don't be surprised if you're the next plaintiff. As with the tobacco industry, it may be only a matter of time before state governments begin to see a direct line between the $1 billion that McDonald's and Burger King spend each year on advertising and their own swelling health care costs.

And I'd say the industry is vulnerable. Fast-food companies are marketing to children a product with proven health hazards and no warning labels. They would do well to protect themselves, and their customers, by providing the nutrition information people need to make informed choices about their products. Without such warnings, we'll see more sick, obese children and more angry, litigious parents. I say, let the deep-fried chips fall where they may.

Hidden Intellectualism

GERALD GRAFF

—◙—

EVERYONE KNOWS SOME young person who is impressively "street smart" but does poorly in school. What a waste, we think, that one who is so intelligent about so many things in life seems unable to apply that intelligence to academic work. What doesn't occur to us, though, is that schools and colleges might be at fault for missing the opportunity to tap into such street smarts and channel them into good academic work.

Nor do we consider one of the major reasons why schools and colleges overlook the intellectual potential of street smarts: the fact that we associate those street smarts with anti-intellectual concerns. We associate the educated life, the life of the mind, too narrowly and exclusively with subjects and texts that we consider inherently weighty and academic. We assume that it's possible to wax intellectual about Plato, Shakespeare, the French Revolution, and nuclear fission, but not about cars, dating, clothing fashions, sports, TV, or video games.

GERALD GRAFF, one of the co-authors of this book, is a professor of English and education at the University of Illinois at Chicago. This piece is adapted from his book *Clueless in Academe: How Schooling Obscures the Life of the Mind*. Copyright © 2003 Yale University.

The trouble with this assumption is that no necessary connection has ever been established between any text or subject and the educational depth and weight of the discussion it can generate. Real intellectuals turn any subject, however lightweight it may seem, into grist for their mill through the thoughtful questions they bring to it, whereas a dullard will find a way to drain the interest out of the richest subject. That's why a George Orwell writing on the cultural meanings of ephemeral penny postcards is infinitely more substantial than the deep cogitations of many professors on Shakespeare or globalization.

Students do need to read models of intellectually challenging writing—and Orwell is a great one—if they are to become intellectuals themselves. But they would be more prone to take on intellectual identities if we encouraged them to do so at first on the subjects that interest them rather than those that interest us.

I offer my own adolescent experience as a case in point. Until I entered college, I hated books and cared only for sports. The only reading I cared to do or could do was sports magazines, on which I became hooked, becoming a regular reader of *Sport* magazine in the late forties, *Sports Illustrated* when it began publishing in 1954, and the annual magazine guides to professional baseball, football, and basketball. I also loved the sports novels for boys of John R. Tunis and Clair Bee and autobiographies of sports stars like Joe DiMaggio's *Lucky to Be a Yankee* and Bob Feller's *Strikeout Story*. In short, I was your typical teenage anti-intellectual—or so I believed for a long time. I have recently come to think, however, that my preference for sports over schoolwork was not anti-intellectualism so much as intellectualism by other means.

In the Chicago neighborhood I grew up in, which had become a melting pot after World War II, our block was solidly middle class, but just a block away—doubtless concentrated there by the real estate companies—were African Americans, Native Americans, and "hillbilly" whites who had recently fled postwar joblessness in the South and Appalachia. Negotiating this class boundary was a tricky matter. On the one hand, it was necessary to maintain the boundary between "clean-cut" boys like me and working-class "hoods," as we called them, which meant that it was good to be openly smart in a bookish sort of way. On the other hand, I was desperate for the approval of the hoods, whom I encountered daily on the playing field and in the neighborhood, and for this purpose it was not at all good to be book-smart. The hoods would turn on you if they sensed you were putting on airs over them: "Who you lookin' at, smart ass?" as a leather-jacketed youth once said to me as he relieved me of my pocket change along with my self-respect.

I grew up torn, then, between the need to prove I was smart and the fear of a beating if I proved it too well; between the need not to jeopardize my respectable future and the need to impress the hoods. As I lived it, the conflict came down to a choice between being physically tough and being verbal. For a boy in my neighborhood and elementary school, only being "tough" earned you complete legitimacy. I still recall endless, complicated debates in this period with my closest pals over who was "the toughest guy in the school." If you were less than negligible as a fighter, as I was, you settled for the next best thing, which was to be inarticulate, carefully hiding telltale marks of literacy like correct grammar and pronunciation.

In one way, then, it would be hard to imagine an adolescence more thoroughly anti-intellectual than mine. Yet in retrospect, I see that it's more complicated, that I and the 1950s themselves were not simply hostile toward intellectualism, but divided and ambivalent. When Marilyn Monroe married the playwright Arthur Miller in 1956 after divorcing the retired baseball star Joe DiMaggio, the symbolic triumph of geek over jock suggested the way the wind was blowing. Even Elvis, according to his biographer Peter Guralnick, turns out to have supported Adlai over Ike in the presidential election of 1956. "I don't dig the intellectual bit," he told reporters. "But I'm telling you, man, he knows the most."

Though I too thought I did not "dig the intellectual bit," I see now that I was unwittingly in training for it. The germs had actually been planted in the seemingly philistine debates about which boys were the toughest. I see now that in the interminable analysis of sports teams, movies, and toughness that my friends and I engaged in—a type of analysis, needless to say, that the real toughs would never have stooped to—I was already betraying an allegiance to the egghead world. I was practicing being an intellectual before I knew that was what I wanted to be.

It was in these discussions with friends about toughness and sports, I think, and in my reading of sports books and magazines, that I began to learn the rudiments of the intellectual life: how to make an argument, weigh different kinds of evidence, move between particulars and generalizations, summarize the views of others, and enter a conversation about ideas. It was in reading and arguing about sports and toughness that I experienced what it felt like to propose a generalization, restate and respond to a counterargument, and perform other intellectualizing operations, including composing the kind of sentences I am writing now.

Only much later did it dawn on me that the sports world was more compelling than school because it was *more intellectual than school*, not less. Sports after all was full of challenging arguments, debates, problems for analysis, and intricate statistics that you could care about, as school conspicuously was not.

I believe that street smarts beat out book smarts in our culture not because street smarts are non-intellectual, as we generally suppose, but because they satisfy an intellectual thirst more thoroughly than school culture, which seems pale and unreal.

They also satisfy the thirst for community. When you entered sports debates, you became part of a community that was not limited to your family and friends, but was national and public. Whereas schoolwork isolated you from others, the pennant race or Ted Williams's .400 batting average was something you could talk about with people you had never met. Sports introduced you not only to a culture steeped in argument, but to a public argument culture that transcended the personal. I can't blame my schools for failing to make intellectual culture resemble the Super Bowl, but I do fault them for failing to learn anything from the sports and entertainment worlds about how to organize and represent intellectual culture, how to exploit its gamelike element and turn it into arresting public spectacle that might have competed more successfully for my youthful attention.

For here is another thing that never dawned on me and is still kept hidden from students, with tragic results: that the real intellectual world, the one that existed in the big world beyond school, is organized very much like the world of team sports, with rival texts, rival interpretations and evaluations of texts, rival theories of why they should be read and taught, and elaborate team competitions in which "fans" of writers, intellectual systems, methodologies, and -isms contend against each other.

To be sure, school contained plenty of competition, which became more invidious as one moved up the ladder (and has become even more so today with the advent of high-stakes testing). In this competition, points were scored not by making arguments, but by a show of information or vast reading, by grade-grubbing, or other forms of oneupmanship. School com-petition, in short, reproduced the less attractive features of sports culture without those that create close bonds and community.

And in distancing themselves from anything as enjoyable and absorbing as sports, my schools missed the opportunity to capitalize on an element of drama and conflict that the intel-lectual world shares with sports. Consequently, I failed to see the parallels between the sports and academic worlds that could have helped me cross more readily from one argument culture to the other.

Sports is only one of the domains whose potential for liter-acy training (and not only for males) is seriously underestimated by educators, who see sports as competing with academic devel-opment rather than a route to it. But if this argument suggests why it is a good idea to assign readings and topics that are close to students' existing interests, it also suggests the limits of this tactic. For students who get excited about the chance to write about their passion for cars will often write as poorly and unre-flectively on that topic as on Shakespeare or Plato. Here is the flip side of what I pointed out before: that there's no necessary relation between the degree of interest a student shows in a text or subject and the quality of thought or expression such a student manifests in writing or talking about it. The challenge, as college professor Ned Laff has put it, "is not simply to exploit students' nonacademic interests, but to get them to see those interests through academic eyes."

To say that students need to see their interests "through aca-demic eyes" is to say that street smarts are not enough. Mak-ing students' nonacademic interests an object of academic study is useful, then, for getting students' attention and overcoming their boredom and alienation, but this tactic won't in itself necessarily move them closer to an academically rigorous treatment of those interests. On the other hand, inviting students to write about cars, sports, or clothing fashions does not have to be a pedagogical cop-out as long as students are required to see these interests "through academic eyes," that is, to think and write about cars, sports, and fashions in a reflective, analytical way, one that sees them as microcosms of what is going on in the wider culture.

If I am right, then schools and colleges are missing an opportunity when they do not encourage students to take their nonacademic interests as objects of academic study. It is self-defeating to decline to introduce any text or subject that figures to engage students who will otherwise tune out academic work entirely. If a student cannot get interested in Mill's *On Liberty* but will read *Sports Illustrated* or *Vogue* or the hip hop magazine *Source* with absorption, this is a strong argument for assigning the magazines over the classic. It's a good bet that if students get hooked on reading and writing by doing term papers on *Source*, they will eventually get to *On Liberty*. But even if they don't, the magazine reading will make them more literate and reflective than they would be otherwise. So it makes pedagogical sense to develop classroom units on sports, cars, fashions, rap music, and other such topics. Give me the student anytime who writes a sharply argued, sociologically acute analysis of an issue of *Source* over the student who writes a lifeless explication of *Hamlet* or Socrates' *Apology*. But again, writing an acute analysis of *Source* means translating one's nonacademic interests into academic terms, turning street smarts into book smarts and recognizing that the two can coexist after all.

The Empire of Images in
Our World of Bodies

SUSAN BORDO

—⌐⌐—

IN OUR SUNDAY news. With our morning coffee. On the bus, in the airport, at the checkout line. It may be a 5 a.m. addiction to the glittering promises of the infomercial: the latest in fat-dissolving pills, miracle hair restoration, makeup secrets of the stars. Or a glancing relationship while waiting at the dentist, trying to distract ourselves from the impending root canal. A teen magazine: tips on how to dress, how to wear your hair, how to make him want you. The endless commercials and advertisements that we believe we pay no attention to.

Constant, everywhere, no big deal. Like water in a goldfish bowl, barely noticed by its inhabitants. Or noticed, but dismissed: "eye candy"—a harmless indulgence. They go down so easily, in and out, digested and forgotten.

Just pictures.

Or perhaps, more accurately, perceptual pedagogy: "How to Interpret Your Body 101." It's become a global requirement; eventually, everyone must enroll. Fiji is just one example. Until

SUSAN BORDO is a professor of English and women's studies at the University of Kentucky. This article was first published in 2003 in *The Chronicle of Higher Education*, Vol. 50, Issue 17. Reprinted with permission of the author.

television was introduced in 1995, the islands had no reported cases of eating disorders. In 1998, three years after programs from the United States and Britain began broadcasting there, 62 percent of the girls surveyed reported dieting. The anthropologist Anne Becker was surprised by the change; she had thought that Fijian aesthetics, which favor voluptuous bodies, would "withstand" the influence of media images. Becker hadn't yet understood that we live in an empire of images and that there are no protective borders.

I am not protected either. I was carded until I was 35. Even when I was 45, people were shocked to learn my age. Young men flirted with me even when I was 50. Having hated my appearance as a child—freckles, Jewish nose, bushy red hair—I was surprised to find myself fairly pleased with it as an adult. Then, suddenly, it all changed. Women at the makeup counter no longer compliment me on my skin. Men don't catch my eye with playful promise in theirs.

I'm 56. The magazines tell me that at this age, a woman can still be beautiful. But they don't mean me. They mean Cher, Goldie, Faye, Candace. Women whose jowls have disappeared as they've aged, whose eyes have become less droopy, lips grown plumper, foreheads smoother with the passing years. They mean Susan Sarandon, who looked older in 1991's *Thelma and Louise* than she does in her movies today. "Aging beautifully" used to mean wearing one's years with style, confidence, and vitality. Today, it means not appearing to age at all. And—like breasts that defy gravity—it's becoming a new bodily norm.

In my 1993 book *Unbearable Weight*, I described the postmodern body, increasingly fed on "fantasies of re-arranging, transforming, and correcting, limitless improvement and change, defying the historicity, the mortality, and, indeed, the very materiality of the body. In place of that materiality, we now have cultural plastic."

When I wrote those words, the most recent statistics, from 1989, listed 681,000 surgical procedures performed. In 2001, 8.5 million procedures were performed. They are cheaper than ever, safer than ever, and increasingly used not for correcting major defects but for "contouring" the face and body. Plastic surgeons seem to have no ethical problem with this. "I'm not here to play philosopher king," said Dr. Randal Haworth in a *Vogue* interview. "I don't have a problem with women who already look good who want to look perfect." Perfect. When did "perfection" become applicable to a human body? The word suggests a Platonic form of timeless beauty—appropriate for marble, perhaps, but not for living flesh.

Greta Van Susteren: former CNN legal analyst, 47 years old. When she had a face-lift, it was a real escalation in the stakes for ordinary women. She had a signature style: no bullshit, a down-to-earth lack of pretense. (During the O.J. trial, she was the only white reporter many black Americans trusted.) Always stylishly dressed and coiffed, she wasn't really pretty. No one could argue that her career was built on her looks. Perhaps quite the opposite. She sent out a subversive message: Brains and personality still count, even on television.

When Greta had her face lifted, another source of inspiration and hope bit the dust. The story was on the cover of *People*, and folks tuned in to her new show on Fox just to see the change—which was significant. But at least she was open about it. The beauties rarely admit they've had "work." Or if they do, it's vague, nonspecific, minimizing of the extent. Cher: "If I'd had as much plastic surgery as people say, there'd be another whole person left over!" OK, so how much have you had? The interviewers accept the silences and evasions. They even embellish the lie. How many interviews have you read that began: "She came into the restaurant looking at least 20 years younger than she is, fresh and relaxed, without a speck of makeup."

This collusion, this myth, that Cher or Goldie or Faye Dunaway, unaltered, is what 50-something looks like today, has altered may face, however—without benefit of surgery. By comparison with theirs, it has become much older than it is.

My expression now appears more serious, too (just what a feminist needs), thanks to the widespread use of Botox. "It's now rare in certain social circles to see a woman over the age of 35 with the ability to look angry," a *New York Times* reporter observed recently. That has frustrated some film directors, like Baz Luhrmann, who directed *Moulin Rouge*. "Their faces can't really move properly," Luhrmann complained. Last week I saw a sign in the beauty parlor where I get my hair cut. "Botox Party! Sign Up!" So my 56-year-old forehead will now be judged against my neighbor's, not just Goldie's, Cher's, and Faye's. On television, a commercial describes the product (which really is a toxin, a dilution of botulism) as "Botox cosmetic." No different from mascara and blush, it's just stuck in with a needle, and it makes your forehead numb.

To add insult to injury, the rhetoric of feminism has been adopted to help advance and justify the industries in anti-aging and body-alteration. Face-lifts, implants, and liposuction are advertised as empowerment, "taking charge" of one's life. "I'm doing it for me" goes the mantra of the talk shows. "Defy your age!" says Melanie Griffith, for Revlon. We're making a revolution, girls. Step right up and get your injections.

Am I immune? Of course not. My bathroom shelves are cluttered with the ridiculously expensive age-defying lotions and potions that beckon to me at the Lancôme and Dior counters. I want my lines, bags, and sags to disappear, and so do the women who can only afford to buy their alphahydroxies at Kmart. There's a limit, though, to what fruit acids can do. As surgeons develop ever more extensive and fine-tuned procedures to correct gravity and erase history from the faces of their patients, the difference between the cosmetically altered and the rest of us grows more and more dramatic.

"The rest of us" includes not only those who resist or are afraid of surgery but the many people who cannot afford basic health care, let alone aesthetic tinkering. As celebrity faces become increasingly more surreal in their wide-eyed, ever-bright agelessness, as *Time* and *Newsweek* (and *Discover* and *Psychology Today*) proclaim that we can now all "stay young forever," the poor continue to sag and wrinkle and lose their teeth. But in the empire of images, where even people in the news for stock scandals or producing septuplets are given instant digital dental work for magazine covers, that is a well-guarded secret. The celebrity testimonials, the advertisements, the beauty columns, all participate in the fiction that the required time, money, and technologies are available to all.

I've been lecturing about media images, eating problems, and our culture of body "enhancement" for nearly 20 years now. Undergraduates frequently make up a large share of my audiences, and they are the ones most likely to "get it." My generation (and older) still refers to "air brushing." Many still believe it is possible to "just turn off the television." They are scornful, disdainful, sure of their own immunity to the world I talk about. No one really believes the ads, do they? Don't we all know those are just images, designed to sell products? Scholars in the audience may trot out theory about cultural resistance and "agency." Men may insist that they love fleshy women.

Fifteen years ago, I felt very alone when my own generation said these things; it seemed that they were living in a different world from the one I was tracking and that there was little hope of bridging the gap. Now, I simply catch the eyes of the 20-year-olds in the audience. They know. They understand that you can be as cynical as you want about the ads—and many of them are—and still feel powerless to resist their messages. They are aware that virtually every advertisement, every magazine cover, has been digitally modified and that very little of what they see is "real." That doesn't stop them from hating their own bodies for failing to live up to computer-generated standards. They know, no matter what their parents, teachers, and clergy are telling them, that "inner beauty" is a big laugh in this culture. If they come from communities that traditionally have celebrated voluptuous bodies and within which food represents love, safety, and home, they may feel isolation and guilt over the widening gap between the values they've grown up with and those tugging at them now.

In the world in which our children are growing up, there is a size zero, and it's a status symbol. The chronic dieters have been at it since they were 8 and 9 years old. They know all about eating disorders; being preached to about the dangers turns them right off. Their world is one in which anorexics swap starvation-diet tips on the Internet, participate in group fasts, offer advice on how to hide your "ana" from family members, and share inspirational photos of emaciated models. But full-blown anorexia has never been the norm among teenage girls; the real epidemic is among the girls with seemingly healthy eating habits, seemingly healthy bodies, who vomit or work their butts off as a regular form of anti-fat maintenance. These girls not only look "normal" but consider themselves normal. The new criterion circulating among teenage girls: If you get rid of it through exercise rather than purging or laxatives, you don't have a problem. Theirs is a world in which groups of dorm girls will plow voraciously through pizzas, chewing and then spitting out each mouthful. Do they have a disorder? Of course not—look, they're eating pizza.

Generations raised in the empire of images are both vulnerable and savvy. They snort when magazines periodically proclaim (about once every six months, the same frequency with which they run cover stories about "starving stars") that in the "new" Hollywood one can be "sexy at any size." They are literati, connoisseurs of the images; they pay close attention to the pounds coming and going—on J. Lo, Reese, Thora, Christina Aguilera, Beyoncé. They know that Kate Winslet, whom the director James Cameron called "Kate Weighs-a-lot" on the set of *Titanic*, was described by the tabloids as "packing on," "ballooning to," "swelling to," "shooting up to," "tipping the scales at" a "walloping," "staggering" weight—of 135 pounds. That slender Courtney Thorne-Smith, who played Calista Flockhart's friend and rival on *Ally McBeal*, quit the show because she could no longer keep up with the pressure to remain as thin as the series creator, David E. Kelley, wanted them to be. That Missy Elliot and Queen Latifah are not on diets just for reasons of health.

I track the culture of young girls today with particular concern, because I'm a mother now. My 4-year-old daughter is a superb athlete with supreme confidence in her body, who prides herself on being able to do anything the boys can do—and better. When I see young girls being diminished and harassed by the culture it feels even more personal to me now. I'm grateful that there's a new generation of female athletes to inspire and support girls like my daughter, Cassie. That our icons are no longer just tiny gymnasts, but powerful soccer, softball, and tennis players, broad-shouldered track stars—Mia Hamm, Sarah Walden, Serena Williams, Marion Jones. During a recent visit to a high school, I saw how the eyes of a 14-year-old athlete shone as she talked about what Marion Jones means to her, and that fills me with hope.

But then, I accidentally tune in to the Maury Povich show, and my heart is torn in two. The topic of the day is "back-to-girl" makeovers. One by one, five beautiful 12-, 13-, and 14-year-old "tomboys" (as Maury called them) are "brought back to their feminine side" (Maury again) through a fashion makeover. We first see them in sweatshirts and caps, insisting that they are as strong as any boy, that they want to dress for comfort, that they're tired of being badgered to look like girls. Why, then, are they submitting to this one-time, on-air transformation? To please their moms. And indeed, as each one is brought back on stage, in full makeup and glamour outfit, hair swinging (and, in the case of the black girls, straightened), striking vampy supermodel "power" poses, their mothers sob as if they had just learned their daughters' cancers were in remission. The moms are so overwhelmed they don't need more, but Maury is clearly bent on complete conversion: "Do you know how pretty you are?" "Look how gorgeous you look!" "Are you going to dress like this more often?" Most of the girls, unsurprisingly, say yes. It's been a frontal assault, there's no room for escape.

As jaded as I am, this Maury show really got to me. I wanted to fold each girl in my arms and get her out of there. Of course, what I really fear is that I won't be able to protect Cassie from the same assault. It's happening already. I watch public-television kids' shows with her and can rarely find fault with the gender-neutral world they portray. We go to Disney movies and see resourceful, spirited heroines. Some of them, like the

Hawaiian girls in *Lilo and Stitch*, even have thick legs and solid bodies. But then, on the way home from the movies, we stop at McDonald's for a Happy Meal, and, despite the fact that Cassie insists she's a boy and wants the boy's toy—a Hot-Wheels car—she is given a box containing a mini-Barbie. Illustrating the box is Barbie's room, and my daughter is given the challenging task of finding all the matching pairs of shoes on the floor.

Later that day, I open a Pottery Barn catalog, browsing for ideas for Cassie's room. The designated boy's room is in primary colors, the bedspread dotted with balls, bats, catching mitts. The caption reads: "I play so many sports that it's hard to pick my favorites." Sounds like my daughter. On the opposite page, the girls' room is pictured, a pastel planetary design. The caption reads: "I like stars because they are shiny." That, too, sounds like my daughter. But Pottery Barn doesn't think a child can inhabit both worlds. If its catalogs were as segregated and stereotyped racially as they are by gender, people would boycott.

I rent a video—*Jimmy Neutron, Boy Genius*—for Cassie. It's marketed as a kids' movie, and the movie is OK for the most part. But then we get to the music video that follows the movie, unaccompanied by any warnings. A group I've never heard of sings a song called "Kids in America." Two of the girls are 13, two are 15, and one is 16—their ages are emblazoned across the screen as each makes her appearance. They are in full vixen attire, with professionally undulating bodies and professionally made-up, come-hither eyes.

Why are we told their ages, I wonder? Are we supposed to be amazed at the illusion of womanhood created by their performance? Or is their youth supposed to make it all right to show this to little kids, a way of saying, "It's only make-believe, only a dress-up game"? It wasn't so long ago that people were outraged by news clips of JonBenet Ramsey performing in children's beauty pageants. In 2002, toddler versions of Britney Spears were walking the streets on Halloween night. Can it really be that we now think dressing our daughters up like tiny prostitutes is cute? That's what the psychologist Sharon Lamb, author of *The Secret Lives of Girls*, thinks. She advises mothers to chill out if their 9-year-old girls "play lovely little games in high heels, strip teasing, flouncing, and jutting their chests out," to relax if their 11-year-olds go out with 'thick blue eye shadow, spaghetti straps and bra straps intertwined, long and leggy with short black dresses." They are "silly and adorable, sexy and marvelous all at once," she tells us, as they "celebrate their objectification," "playing out male fantasies . . . but without risk."

Without risk? I have nothing against girls playing dress-up. But flouncing is one thing; strip teasing is another. Thick blue eye shadow in mommy's bathroom is fine; an 11-year-old's night on the town is not. Reading those words "without risk," I want to remind Sharon Lamb that 22 to 29 percent of all rapes against girls occur when they are 11 and younger. We might like to think that those rapes are the work of deranged madmen, so disconnected from reality as to be oblivious to the culture around them. Or that all we need to do to protect our daughters is simply teach them not to take candy from or go into cars with strangers. The reality, however, is that young girls are much more likely to be raped by friends and family members than by strangers and that very few men, whether strangers or acquaintances, are unaffected by a visual culture of nymphets prancing before their eyes, exuding a sexual knowledge and experience that preteens don't really have. Feminists used to call this "rape culture." We never hear that phrase anymore.

Still, progressive forces are not entirely asleep in the empire of images. I think of YM teen magazine, for example. After conducting a survey that revealed that 86 percent of its young readers were dissatisfied with the way their bodies looked, YM openly declared war on eating disorders and body-image problems, instituting an editorial policy against the publishing of diet pieces and deliberately seeking out full-size models—without identifying them as such—for all its fashion spreads. A colleague suggested that this resistance to the hegemony of the fat-free body may have something to do with the fact that the editors are young enough to have studied feminism and cultural studies while they got their B.A.'s in English and journalism.

Most progressive developments in the media, of course, are driven by market considerations rather than social conscience. So, for example, the fact that 49 million women are size 12 or more is clearly the motive behind new, flesh-normalizing campaigns created by "Just My Size" and Lane Bryant. Ad campaigns for these lines of clothing proudly show off zaftig bodies in sexy underwear and, unlike older marketing to "plus size" women, refuse to use that term, insisting (accurately) that what has been called plus size is in fact average. It's a great strategy for making profits, but a species of resistance nonetheless. "I won't allow myself to be invisible anymore," these ads proclaim, on our behalf. "But I won't be made visible as a cultural oddity or a joke, either, because I'm not. I'm the norm."

The amorality of consumer capitalism, in its restless search for new markets and new ways to generate and feed desire, has also created a world of racial representations that are far more diverse now than when I wrote *Unbearable Weight*. This is another issue that has acquired special meaning for me, because my daughter is biracial, and I am acutely aware of the world that she sees and what it is telling her about herself. Leafing through current magazines, noting the variety of skin tones, noses, mouths depicted there, I'm glad, for the moment, that Cassie is growing up today rather than in the '70s, when Cheryl Tiegs ruled. It's always possible, of course, to find things that are still "wrong" with these representations; racist codes and aesthetics die hard. The Jezebels and geishas are still with us; and, although black male models and toddlers are allowed to have locks and "naturals," straight hair—straighter nowadays than I ever thought it was possible for anyone's hair to be— seems almost mandatory for young black women.

It's easy, too, to be cynical. Today's fashionable diversity is brought to us, after all, by the same people who brought us the hegemony of the blue-eyed blonde and who've made wrinkles and cellulite into diseases. It's easy to dismiss fashion's current love affair with full lips and biracial children as a shameless attempt to exploit ethnic markets while providing ethnic chic for white beauty tourists. Having a child, however, has given me another perspective, as I try to imagine how the models look through her eyes. Cassie knows nothing about the motives of the people who've produced the images. At her age, she can only take them at face value. And at face value, they present a world that includes and celebrates her, as the world that I grew up in did not include and celebrate me. For all my anger, cynicism, and frustration with our empire of images, I cannot help but be grateful for that.

And sometimes, surveying the plastic, digitalized world of bodies that are the norm now, I am convinced that our present state of enchantment is just a moment away from revulsion, or perhaps simply boredom. I see a 20-something woman dancing at a local outdoor swing party, her tummy softly protruding over the thick leather belt of her low-rider jeans. Not taut, not toned, not artfully camouflaged like some unsightly deformity, but proudly, sensuously displayed, reminding me of Madonna in the days before she became the sinewy dominatrix. Is it possible that we are beginning to rebel against the manufactured look of celebrity bodies, beginning to be repelled by their armored perfection?

Such hopeful moments, I have to admit, are fleeting. Usually, I feel horrified. I am sharply aware that expressing my horror openly nowadays invites being thought of as a preachy prude, a relic of an outmoded feminism. At talks to young audiences, I try to lighten my touch, celebrate the positive, make sure that my criticisms of our culture are not confused with being anti-beauty, anti-fitness, or anti-sex. But I also know that when parents and teachers become fully one with the culture, children are abandoned to it. I don't tell them to love their bodies or turn off the television—useless admonitions today, and ones I cannot obey myself—but I do try to disrupt, if only temporarily, their everyday immersion in the culture. For just an hour or so, I won't let it pass itself off simply as "normalcy."

The lights go down, the slides go up. For just a moment, we confront how bizarre, how impossible, how contradictory the images are. We laugh together over Oprah's head digitally grafted to another women's body, at the ad for breast implants in which the breasts stick straight up in the air. We gasp together as the before and after photos of Jennifer Lopez are placed side by side. We cheer for Marion Jones's shoulders, boo the fact that WNBA Barbie is just the same old Barbie, but with a basketball in her hand. For just a moment, we are in charge of the impact the faked images of "perfect" bodies have on us.

We look at them together and share—just for a moment—outrage.

INDEX OF TEMPLATES

—▫—

INTRODUCING WHAT "THEY SAY" *(p. 21)*

▸ A number of sociologists have recently suggested that X's work has several fundamental problems.

▸ It has become common today to dismiss X's contribution to the field of sociology.

▸ In their recent work, Y and Z have offered harsh critiques of Dr. X for _____.

INTRODUCING "STANDARD VIEWS" *(p. 22)*

▸ Americans today tend to believe that _____.

▸ Conventional wisdom has it that _____.

▸ Common sense seems to dictate that _____.

▸ The standard way of thinking about topic X has it that _____.

▸ It is often said that _____.

▸ My whole life I have heard it said that _____.

▸ You would think that _____.

▸ Many people assumed that _____.

MAKING WHAT "THEY SAY" SOMETHING *YOU* SAY *(pp. 22–23)*

▶ I've always believed that _____ .

▶ When I was a child, I used to think that _____ .

▶ Although I should know better by now, I cannot help thinking that

_____ .

▶ At the same time that I believe _____ , I also believe _____ .

INTRODUCING SOMETHING IMPLIED OR ASSUMED *(p. 23)*

▶ Although none of them have ever said so directly, my teachers have often given me the impression that _____ .

▶ One implication of X's treatment of _____ is that _____ .

▶ Although X does not say so directly, she apparently assumes that _____ .

▶ While they rarely admit as much, _____ often take for granted that _____ .

INTRODUCING AN ONGOING DEBATE *(p. 24)*

▶ In discussions of X, one controversial issue has been _____ . On the one hand, _____ argues _____ . On the other hand, _____ contends _____ . Others even maintain _____ . My own view is _____ .

▶ When it comes to the topic of _____, most of us will readily agree that _____. Where this agreement usually ends, however, is on the question of _____. Whereas some are convinced that _____, others maintain that _____.

▶ In conclusion, then, as I suggested earlier, defenders of_____ can't have it both ways. Their assertion that _____ is contradicted by their claim that _____.

INTRODUCING SUMMARIES AND QUOTATIONS *(pp. 36–37)*

▶ X acknowledges that _____.

▶ X agrees that _____.

▶ X argues that _____.

▶ X believes that _____.

▶ X denies/does not deny that _____.

▶ X claims that _____.

▶ X complains that _____.

▶ X concedes that _____.

▶ X demonstrates that _____.

▶ X deplores the tendency to _____.

▶ X celebrates the fact that _____.

▶ X emphasizes that _____.

- ▸ X insists that _____.

- ▸ X observes that _____.

- ▸ X questions whether _____.

- ▸ X refutes the claim that _____.

- ▸ X reminds us that _____.

- ▸ X reports that _____.

- ▸ X suggests that _____.

- ▸ X urges us to _____.

INTRODUCING QUOTATIONS *(p. 43)*

- ▸ X states, "_____."

- ▸ As the prominent philosopher X puts it, "_____."

- ▸ According to X, "_____."

- ▸ X himself writes, "_____."

- ▸ In her book, _____, X maintains that "_____"

- ▸ Writing in the journal *Commentary*, X complains that "_____."

- ▸ In X's view, "_____."

- ▸ X agrees when she writes, "_____."

- ▸ X disagrees when he writes, "_____."

- ▸ X complicates matters further when he writes, "_____."

Index of Templates

EXPLAINING QUOTATIONS *(p. 44)*

▶ Basically, X is saying _____.

▶ In other words, X believes _____.

▶ In making this comment, X argues that _____.

▶ X is insisting that _____.

▶ X's point is that _____.

▶ The essence of X's argument is that _____.

DISAGREEING, WITH REASONS *(p. 55)*

▶ I think X is mistaken because she overlooks _____.

▶ X's claim that _____ rests upon the questionable assumption that _____.

▶ I disagree with X's view that _____ because, as recent research has shown, _____.

▶ X contradicts herself/can't have it both ways. On the one hand, she argues _____. But on the other hand, she also says _____.

▶ By focusing on _____, X overlooks the deeper problem of _____.

▶ X claims _____, but we don't need him to tell us that. Anyone familiar with _____ has long known that _____.

AGREEING—WITH A DIFFERENCE *(p. 57)*

▶ I agree that _____ because my experience _____ confirms it.

▶ X surely is right about _____ because, as she may not be aware, recent studies have shown that _____.

▶ X's theory of _____ is extremely useful because it sheds insight on the difficult problem of _____.

▶ I agree that _____, a point that needs emphasizing since so many people believe _____.

▶ Those unfamiliar with this school of thought may be interested to know that it basically boils down to _____.

▶ If group X is right that _____, as I think they are, then we need to reassess the popular assumption that _____.

AGREEING AND DISAGREEING SIMULTANEOUSLY *(pp. 59–61)*

▶ Although I agree with X up to a point, I cannot accept his overall conclusion that _____.

▶ Although I disagree with much that X says, I fully endorse his final conclusion that _____.

▶ Though I concede that _____, I still insist that _____.

▶ Whereas X provides ample evidence that _____, Y and Z's research on _____ and _____ convinces me that _____ instead.

Index of Templates

- X is right that _____, but she seems on more dubious ground when she claims that _____.

- While X is probably wrong when she claims that _____, she is right that _____.

- I'm of two minds about X's claim that _____. On the one hand, I agree that _____. On the other hand, I'm not sure if _____.

- My feelings on the issue are mixed. I do support X's position that _____, but I find Y's argument about _____ and Z's research on _____ to be equally persuasive.

SIGNALING WHO IS SAYING WHAT *(p. 67)*

- X argues _____.

- According to both X and Y, _____.

- Politicians _____, X argues, should _____.

- Most athletes will tell you that _____.

- My own view, however, is that _____.

- I agree, as X may not realize, that _____.

- But _____ are real and, arguably, the most significant factor in _____.

- But X is wrong that _____.

- However, it is simply not true that _____.

- Indeed, it is highly likely that _____.

▸ But the view that _____ does not fit all the facts.

▸ X is right that _____.

▸ X is wrong that _____.

▸ X is both right and wrong that _____.

▸ Yet a sober analysis of the matter reveals _____.

▸ Nevertheless, new research shows _____.

▸ Anyone familiar with _____ should see that _____.

EMBEDDING VOICE MARKERS *(pp. 70–71)*

▸ X overlooks what I consider an important point about _____.

▸ My own view is that what X insists is a _____ is in fact a _____.

▸ I wholeheartedly endorse what X calls _____.

▸ These conclusions, which X discusses in _____, add weight to the argument that _____.

ENTERTAINING OBJECTIONS *(p. 78)*

▸ At this point I would like to raise some objections that have been inspired by the skeptic in me. She feels that I have been ignoring _____. "_____," she says to me, "_____."

▸ Yet some readers may challenge the view that _____. After all, many believe _____. Indeed, my own argument that _____ seems to ignore _____ and _____.

▸ Of course, many will probably disagree with this assertion that _____.

NAMING YOUR NAYSAYERS *(p. 79)*

▸ Here many *feminists* would probably object that _____.

▸ But *social Darwinists* would certainly take issue with the argument that _____.

▸ *Biologists*, of course, may want to dispute my claim that _____.

▸ Nevertheless, both *followers and critics of Malcom X* will probably argue that _____.

▸ Although not all *Christians* think alike, some of them will probably dispute my claim that _____.

▸ *Non-native English speakers* are so diverse in their views that it's hard to generalize about them, but some are likely to object on the grounds that _____.

INTRODUCING OBJECTIONS INFORMALLY *(p. 80)*

▸ But is my proposal realistic? What are the chances of its actually being adopted?

▶ Yet is it always true that _____? Is it always the case, as I have been suggesting, that _____?

▶ However, does the evidence I've cited prove conclusively that _____?

▶ "Impossible," you say. "Your evidence must be skewed."

MAKING CONCESSIONS WHILE STILL STANDING YOUR GROUND *(p. 85)*

▶ Although I grant that _____, I still maintain that _____.

▶ Proponents of X are right to argue that _____. But they exaggerate when they claim that _____.

▶ While it is true that _____, it does not necessarily follow that _____.

▶ On the one hand, I agree with X that _____. But on the other hand, I still insist that _____.

INDICATING WHO CARES *(p. 91)*

▶ _____ used to think _____. But recently [or within the past few decades] _____ suggests that _____.

▶ What this new research does, then, is correct the mistaken impression, held by many earlier researchers, that _____.

▶ These findings challenge the work of earlier researchers, who tended to assume that _____.

▸ Recent studies like these shed new light on _____, which previous studies had not addressed.

▸ Researchers have long assumed that _____. For instance, one eminent scholar of cell biology, _____, assumed in _____, her seminal work on cell structures and functions, that fat cells _____. As _____ herself put it, "_____" (200-). Another leading scientist, _____, argued that fat cells "_____" (200-). Ultimately, when it came to the nature of fat, the basic assumption was that _____.

But a new body of research shows that fat cells are far more complex and that _____.

▸ If sports enthusiasts stopped to think about it, many of them might simply assume that the most successful athletes _____. However, new research shows _____.

▸ These findings challenge dieters' common assumptions that _____.

▸ At first glance, teenagers appear to _____. But on closer inspection _____.

ESTABLISHING WHY YOUR CLAIMS MATTER *(pp. 94–95)*

▸ X matters/is important because _____.

▸ Although X may seem trivial, it is in fact crucial in terms of today's concern over _____.

▸ Ultimately, what is at stake here is _____.

- These findings have important consequences for the broader domain of _____.

- My discussion of X is in fact addressing the larger matter of _____.

- These conclusions/This discovery will have significant applications in _____ as well as in _____.

- Although X may seem of concern to only a small group of _____, it should in fact concern anyone who cares about _____.

COMMONLY USED TRANSITIONS

Cause and Effect

accordingly	since
as a result	so
consequently	then
hence	therefore
it follows, then	thus

Conclusion

as a result	so
consequently	the upshot of all this is that
hence	therefore
in conclusion, then	thus
in short	to sum up
in sum, then	to summarize
it follows, then	

Comparison

along the same lines	likewise
in the same way	similarly

Index of Templates

Contrast
although	nevertheless
but	nonetheless
by contrast	on the contrary
conversely	on the other hand
despite the fact that	regardless
even though	whereas
however	while
in contrast	yet

Addition
also	in fact
and	indeed
besides	moreover
furthermore	so too
in addition	

Concession
admittedly	of course
although it is true that	naturally
granted	to be sure
I concede that	

Example
after all	for instance
as an illustration	specifically
consider	to take a case in point
for example	

Elaboration
actually	to put it another way
by extension	to put it bluntly
in short	to put it succinctly
that is	ultimately
in other words	

ADDING METACOMMENTARY *(pp. 128–30)*

- In other words, _____.

- What _____ really means by this is _____.

- My point is _____.

- Essentially, I am arguing that _____.

- My point is not that we should _____, but that we should _____.

- What _____ really means is _____.

- In other words, _____.

- To put it another way, _____.

- In sum, then, _____.

- My conclusion, then, is that, _____.

- In short, _____.

- What is more important, _____.

- Incidentally, _____.

- By the way, _____.

- Chapter 2 explores _____, while Chapter 3 examines _____.

- Having just argued that _____, let us now turn our attention to _____.

- Although some readers may object that _____, I would answer that _____.

Acknowledgments

—⊡—

We have our superb editor, Marilyn Moller, to thank for this book. It was Marilyn who first encouraged us to write it, and she has devoted herself tirelessly to helping us at every stage of the process. We never failed to benefit from her incisive suggestions, her unfailing patience, and her cheerful good humor.

Our thanks go as well to John Darger, Norton's Chicago representative, who also offered early encouragement to write this book; to Alice Vigliani, for her astute copyediting; to Maggie Wagner, for the striking design; to Diane O'Connor, for her superb management of the production process; to Debra Morton-Hoyt, for her excellent work on the cover; and to Cat Spencer, for helping with many things large and small.

We owe special thanks to our colleagues in the English department at the University of Illinois at Chicago: Walter Benn Michaels, our department head, and Ann Feldman, Director of University Writing Programs, for encouraging us to teach first-year composition courses at UIC in which we could try out ideas and drafts of our manuscript. Tom Moss, Diane Chin, and Matt Pavesich have also been very supportive of our efforts. We are especially grateful to Ann and Diane for bringing us into their graduate course on the teaching of writing, and to Ann, Tom, Diane, and Matt for inviting us to present our ideas in UIC's Mile 8 workshops for writing instructors.

The encouragement, suggestions, and criticisms we received at these sessions have proved invaluable.

We are also especially grateful to Steve Benton and Nadya Pittendrigh, who taught a section of composition with us using an early draft of this book. Steve made many helpful suggestions, particularly regarding the exercises. We are grateful to Andy Young, a lecturer at UIC who has tested our book in his courses and who gave us extremely helpful feedback. And we thank Vershawn A. Young, whose work on code-meshing influenced our argument in Chapter 9, and Hillel Crandus, whose classroom handout inspired our appendix, "Entering Classroom Discussions."

We are grateful to the many colleagues and friends who've let us talk our ideas out with them and given extremely helpful responses. UIC's former dean, Stanley Fish, has been central in this respect, both in personal conversations and in his incisive articles calling for greater focus on form in the teaching of writing. Our conversations with Jane Tompkins have also been integral to this book, as was the composition course that Jane co-taught with Gerald entitled "Can We Talk?" Lenny Davis, too, offered both intellectual insight and emotional support, as did Heather Arnet, Jennifer Ashton, Janet Atwill, Kyra Auslander, Noel Barker, Jim Benton, Jack Brereton, Tim Cantrick, David Chinitz, Lisa Chinitz, Pat Chu, Bridget O'Rourke Flisk, Steve Flisk, Gwynne Gertz, Judy Gardiner, Howard Gardner, Ben Hale, Scott Hammerl, Patricia Harkin, Andy Hoberek, John Huntington, Joe Janangelo, Paul Jay, David Jolliffe, Jo Liebermann, Maurice J. Meilleur, Greg Meyerson, Alan Meyers, Anna Minkov, Chris Newfield, Jim Phelan, Paul Psilos, Charles Ross, Evan Seymour, Eileen Seifert, David Shumway, Herb Simons, Jim Sosnoski, Chuck Venegoni,

Virginia Wexman, Jeffrey Williams, Lynn Woodbury, and the late Wayne Booth, whose friendship we dearly miss.

We are grateful for having had the opportunity to present our ideas at a number of campuses: Augustana College, Brandeis University, Bryn Mawr College, University of Delaware, Duke University, Duquesne University, Elmhurst College, Furman University, Harper College, Haverford College, Illinois State University, the Lawrenceville School, New Trier High School, Northern Michigan University, North Carolina A & T University, University of Notre Dame, University of Rochester, University of South Florida, St. Andrew's School, St. Charles High School, Swarthmore College, and the University of Wisconsin at Whitewater.

We particularly thank those who helped arrange these visits and discussed writing issues with us: Pramod Mishra and Jeff Abernathy at Augustana; Joe Harris and Van Hillard at Duke; Greg Barnheisel, Linda Kinnahan, and Albert Labriola at Duquesne; Margaret Oakes and Emily Poe at Furman; Tom Deans at Haverford; Chris Breu, Ronald Fortune, Elizabeth Hatmaker, Ron Strickland, and Doug Hesse at Illinois State; Trig Thoreson at Harper; Dominick Randolph at Lawrenceville; John Cadwell, Cathy D'Agostino, and John O'Connor at New Trier High; Jody Trost at Northern Michigan; Connie Mick at Notre Dame; Deborah Rossen-Knill at Rochester; Dean Georg Kleine, Gary Olson, and Lynn Worsham at South Florida; John Austin at St. Andrew's; David Jones at St. Charles; and Dean Howard Ross at Wisconsin.

For inviting us to present our ideas at their conferences, we are grateful to Wendy Katkin, Director of the Reinvention Center of SUNY Stony Brook; Luchen Li of the Michigan English Association; and Lisa Lee and Barbara Ransby of the Public Square in Chicago. Thanks also to our friend Don Lazere for including us in a panel at the annual convention of the Modern Language Association.

A very special thanks also goes to those who reviewed this manuscript for Norton; their suggestions contributed enormously to this book: Alan Ainsworth (Houston Community College); Rise Axelrod (University of California, Riverside); Bob Baron (Mesa Community College); David Bartholomae (University of Pittsburgh); Diane Belcher (Georgia State University); Michel De Benedictis (Miami Dade College); Joseph Bizup (Columbia University); Patricia Bizzell (College of the Holy Cross); John Brereton (Harvard University); Richard Bullock (Wright State University); Charles Cooper (University of California, San Diego); Christine Cozzens (Agnes Scott College); Sarah Duerden (Arizona State University); Russel Durst (University of Cincinnati); Joseph Harris (Duke University); Paul Heilker (Virginia Polytechnic Institute); Michael Hennessy (Texas State University); Karen Lunsford (University of California, Santa Barbara); Libby Miles (University of Rhode Island); Mike Rose (University of California, Los Angeles); William H. Smith (Weatherford College); Scott Stevens (Western Washington University); Patricia Sullivan (University of Colorado); Pamela Wright (University of California, San Diego); Daniel Zimmerman (Middlesex Community College).

Finally, we are grateful to David Bartholomae, who suggested our book's subtitle.

GERALD GRAFF, a Professor of English and Education at the University of Illinois at Chicago, has had a major impact on teachers through such books as *Professing Literature: An Institutional History, Beyond the Culture Wars: How Teaching the Conflicts Can Revitalize American Education*, and, most recently, *Clueless in Academe: How Schooling Obscures the Life of the Mind*. He will be President of the Modern Language Association of America in 2008. CATHY BIRKENSTEIN, who first developed the templates used in this book, is a Lecturer in English at the University of Illinois at Chicago. She recently received her PhD in American literature and is currently working on two projects, one on academic literacy and another on the discourse of American democracy. Together Gerald and Cathy direct UIC's Writing-in-the-Disciplines Program and conduct campus workshops on writing. They live with their son, Aaron, in Chicago.

PHOTOGRAPH BY ERIC BIRKENSTEIN